GRIEF
WARRIOR

Hardcover ISBN: 978-1-0879-0489-4
Paperback ISBN: 978-1-955546-07-2

A Publication of *Tall Pine Books* | tallpinebooks.com

*Published in the United States of America

GRIEF WARRIOR

A JOURNEY OF HOPE AND COURAGE
TO THE OTHER SIDE OF TRAUMATIC LOSS

CINDY BAUMANN

"Cindy Baumann has had more tragedies in her life than most people. I cannot imagine the trauma of nursing a small child through cancer and then, after the cancer being in remission for years, having him die in a hunting accident when he was 26, just months after his marriage and when he was on the way to becoming a doctor. Cindy invites you into her family in an authentic, loving way. You get to know her and her son Shaun and everyone else so that you feel like you belong. When everything feels dark and hopeless, Cindy, through her writing, gently takes your hand and leads you through to the other side to find love, life, and renewed joy. Her faith is strong, and she allows you to lean on her and her experience as she shows you a way through your own grief. Shaun is a bright light even in death, and I am grateful that I have gotten to know him through Cindy's loving heart. I am also grateful for having had the opportunity to read *Grief Warrior*."

—JAN WARNER
Author of *Grief Day by Day*
www.Facebook.com/GriefSpeaksOut

"Grief is gritty, and so is this memoir. After multiple life traumas, including her son's death, author Cindy Baumann had a battle on her hands...one that required her to become a grief warrior. Faced with debilitating depression, panic disorder, and suicidal thoughts, she had no choice but to fight. *Grief Warrior* leads us through her dark journey, revealing what the underbelly of grief really feels like to a mother who suffers the ultimate loss, and yet it remains a story of great inspiration. A brave account of both gut-wrenching pain and the exploration of traditional and unique methods of healing, it offers hope to the hopeless. I believe the candor, courage, and wisdom within its pages will give strength to many grieving hearts."

—GARY ROE
Author of *Shattered: Surviving the Loss of a Child*

"The author of this remarkable book has had more than her share of loss in her life. Just when she began to see a glimmer of hope, her world fell apart again...and again...and again. This is a must-read for anyone who has ever experienced grief, no matter what kind, no matter how many times. Why? Because it courageously reveals how you, too, can rise above your lowest depths by acknowledging the insights you gain from your loss. That's what a grief warrior is. That is what you, too, can become."

—ALLEN KLEIN
Author of *Embracing Life After Loss*

"Grief Warrior captures the raw, uncensored reality of living with heart-shattering loss. Highly relatable for anyone coping with the traumatic loss of a loved one, this moving book makes you feel not so alone in your grief. Author Cindy Baumann, who lost her beloved son, demonstrates that through loss comes the ability to grow, adapt, and discover a new way of being in the world. What is possible for her is possible for you. Begin healing from loss, and pick up a copy of this book today. "

—CHELSEA HANSON
Author of *The Sudden Loss Survival Guide*

"Some years ago, in the midst of her debilitating grief, Cindy Baumann reached out to me for help. I shared with her my experiences with soul writing, and she incorporated this method into her healing process. In Grief Warrior, she describes how this powerful tool can provide messages from the Divine, our departed loved ones, and our inner selves to help us navigate through the raging waters of grief. "

—JANET CONNER
Author of *Writing Down Your Soul*

Dedicated to:

To my sons Ryan, Jordan, and Justin... you each hold a precious place in my heart. You knew I loved you when I couldn't see past my grief, and for that I am forever grateful. And, to my husband Kevin... thank you for never giving up on me even after I gave up on myself. I love you all, with my whole heart and soul.

To my son Shaun, who taught me so much about love, compassion, and selflessness during his time on Earth. My love is always with you Shaun, and I believe you still teach me from your broader perspective in heaven. I will miss you until I take my last breath and embrace you once again.

SHAUN LYNN WINTER
September 8, 1981 – November 24, 2007

CONTENTS

FOREWORD

IMAGINE LIFE IS a board game. A bit like Monopoly. You roll the dice. You move around the board. You land on a square. Each square represents a life experience.

In the game of life, there are some squares you want to land on like, "falling in love," "celebrating a birthday," "getting married," "jumping in puddles," "living your purpose," "a new pair of shoes," "going on an adventure," and "becoming a parent." It feels good to be alive when you land on squares like these.

There are also squares in the game of life that you hope to avoid like "failing a school exam," "financial poverty," "being discriminated against," "a serious illness," "heartbreak hotel," "miss a flight," "go to jail," "lose your money," "get a divorce," "out of work," and "death of a loved one."

"Death of a loved one." There isn't a soul alive who'd choose to land on this square. And yet, in the game of life, you can't avoid it forever. At some point you will land on a square like "having a miscarriage," "stillbirth," "attending a funeral," "losing a grandparent," "becoming a widow," and even "burying your son or daughter."

Grief is inevitable when you play the game of life. Everyone hopes to avoid it, but grief comes too soon for all of us. To play the game of life well—to live it wholeheartedly until your dying breath—you have to learn how to grieve.

You have to become a grief warrior—like Cindy Baumann, who is the author of this precious book that you hold in your hands.

Cindy and I first started corresponding about ten years ago, not long after the death of her beloved son Shaun. In her first email to me, Cindy asked me for any advice I had on how to grieve well.

Here's how I began my reply to Cindy: "Dear Cindy, I am so sorry to hear about your loss. I have two young children of my own, and I honestly can barely begin to imagine what you must have been through. That said, I do know a thing or two about grief. The first thing is, you must give it all of your attention."

Grief gets worse the more you try to avoid it. You can't make it go away by avoiding it. By trying to avoid grief, you can't mourn properly. Only by turning towards grief, and giving it your full attention, can you learn to live with loss, and live in such a way that truly honours the life of a loved one.

Grieving alone is impossible. A grief warrior knows that help is essential on the journey. You mustn't ever try to grieve alone. It's only by sharing our grief that we learn to live with it.

Cindy Baumann shares her grief with us in her book *Grief Warrior*. She writes with painstaking honesty. Her emotional honesty delivers spiritual healing and wisdom in abundance. You will see what I mean when you turn the pages of Cindy's gift to us.

Cindy found a way to befriend her grief. She even appointed grief as her teacher. She has learned that in the game of life, the physical form of relationships always changes, but that souls stay in relationship forever, and that love never ends.

Thank you, Cindy, for sharing your journey with us. Thank you for helping us to grieve well, to live well, and to love well.

—ROBERT HOLDEN, Ph.D.
Author of *Finding Love Everywhere*
London, December 31, 2020

INTRODUCTION

When the unthinkable happens, the lighthouse is hope.
Once we choose hope, everything is possible.
—Christopher Reeve

IN MY WILDEST dreams, I never thought I would be where I am to-day—sitting at a desk writing a book about my journey through grief. A huge part of me died the day my son was killed. For so many years, I wanted to join him in death, and I often considered taking my life. It seemed pointless for me to go on.

My life felt suspended between two worlds—the non-physical and the physical. I couldn't be there, but I sure didn't want to be here. It wasn't that I had nothing to live for, because I did. I had a wonderful husband, three terrific sons, a supportive daughter-in-law, the sweetest granddaughter, and a thriving career. But along with my blessings was a constant feeling of anguish over the tragic way Shaun died. The pain of his loss overshadowed everything else in my life. It was so intense, I thought I would die of a broken heart.

Getting through each day was a long, lonely struggle. The days, weeks, and years I spent in this state of grief seemed to take an eternity to pass. Losing my son challenged every ounce of faith I'd ever had. My feelings about life, spirituality, and God lurched between extremes of hope and hatred. When I was sitting in church, listening to the priest harp on about forgiveness, I wanted to scream at the top of my lungs right in the middle of the sermon. I'd watch while the good people and the sinners sat with their hands in their lap in repose, feeling the vulgar language my mom had taught me not to use rising in my throat. I wanted to hurl the worst words you can imagine, like projectile vomit, at everyone.

I searched everywhere for something that would help me move through the state I was in. I drank too much and didn't care and tried to hurt myself in ways I never thought I could stoop to. I'd wake in the morning drowsy, and with hardly enough energy to pull myself out of bed, sit on the toilet with my elbows on my knees and hands cupped over my eyes, and try to pretend it hadn't happened. Next, I'd head to the kitchen and pour a strong cup of coffee, eat a piece of dry toast, and take an aspirin to curb my headache . . . all so I could start another long day without my son. I wanted so much to believe it wasn't true, that half the time I lived in a fantasy world where Shaun had returned.

To me, grief was like a wide, angry river, full of rough waves and dangerous currents that could exhaust the strongest swimmer. I knew I had to cross it if I were going to survive. It was either that or drown trying. Every time I made a little progress, it seemed like another whirlpool would suck me back under. I'd manage to break free from the current and take a few strokes, and then it would start all over again. I wanted to give up, but I didn't. It took many tries to make it across that river. Through sheer grit and perseverance, I survived and found a new life on a new shore. As a result, I have some tools to share with others who are suffering as I did. I pray that you will find in my story something you can hold on to as you process your own journey through grief.

CHAPTER ONE

FLASHBACK

If you are going through hell—keep going.
—Winston Churchill

MY SON SHAUN fought a long battle with an aggressive cancer as a baby. He went through years of chemotherapy treatment, radiation, and many surgeries, but against all odds, he survived. Living through that period of my life was difficult, but in the end, I still had my son. When the doctors declared the cancer was gone, I thought we had won the battle and could keep him forever. We'd fought so hard to save him, it didn't seem possible that something else would take him from us. Losing him to an accidental gunshot wound decades later was for me the ultimate loss.

The shock of Shaun's passing magnified all the other traumas I'd gone through in my life. There had been so very many. The only way I'd been able to cope was to mentally stuff them into a box and put them high up on a shelf in the closet of my mind. When I was forced to open the door to that closet, they all came tumbling down. Under the weight of all those traumas, I became paralyzed in my grief.

Therapy was one way I tried to cope with the panic and sadness I dealt with on a daily basis. I kept a journal of some of these sessions; here's one that describes one of the most intense sessions I experienced:

I throw on a pair of jeans and a sweater and head to my counseling session, shaking like a leaf. I know my therapist expects me to revisit the worst day of my life, and I doubt my ability to go through with it. I've done everything I can to avoid dealing with the intrusive memories, emotional triggers, and depression that I've lived with for six years. The last thing I want to do is dredge it all up again. All my instincts tell me to bolt. I stay for one reason—I am desperate to heal.

There is no hiding my panic from the professional. Every inhalation feels as though it could be my last. He explains the new therapy he wants to try with me. It's called EMDR or Eye Movement Desensitization Reprocessing. I tremble as he describes it. I do everything I can to remain composed, but I can feel the memories crowding in. Tears fill my eyes—I know where I'm heading. My chest is tight, and I can't catch my breath. I have to force myself to sit down on the cold leather couch. My right hand is clenched, and my left is ready to reach for the door in case I have to run.

As the sessions starts, my thoughts take me to an image of the body of my son Shaun lying on the cold ground, covered with a dusting of snow. This isn't a memory, because I wasn't there when Shaun was shot, but I've been told the details by those who were present. In searching for comfort, I made them tell me every excruciating detail, and those forced recountings have haunted me ever since.

He lies in a stretch of woods where most of the leaves have already fallen to the ground in preparation for winter. In my mind's eye, I can see his big brother, Ryan, bending over him, desperately trying to breathe life into him. As he puts his mouth against Shaun's, his tears fall to the ground, and the warmth melts the snow around Shaun's face. Ryan pours every ounce of energy he has into his brother, giving his all to save him. The feeling of helplessness running through Ryan's heart tramples through mine.

My crying intensifies and my breathing is shallow. I feel like I'm suffocating. My therapist reminds me to breathe deeply, but I go into another panic attack. I'm getting sick and he moves the wastebasket closer. I wish I could vomit out the grief living inside me. The sensation inside of me is unbearable. My legs won't stop moving, as if they have a mind of their own. My feet start rubbing hard against my shins, making them raw and sore. My therapist continues, but my body writhes in an attempt to escape it.

When the agonizing memories burst free, they attack me with a vengeance. First, I'm hit with a wave of guilt. I wasn't there to rescue him from the cold ground. I couldn't hold him as he died. I'm so sorry I couldn't hold him in my arms when he needed me. I miss him so much; it's eating me alive. I blame myself. Could I have stopped him from going that day? I wasn't home when he left—I hate myself for that. I was out shopping with my sisters and having fun at my friend's party.

Shaun had called me to see how my day went. I remember his voice that day, so bright and happy. "Mom, was Roger excited?" he said. "What did he think?" Then he called me again later. I was in the shoe department at a local store. "What are you doing, Mom?" he said playfully.

That's the last time I talked to him. If only we could've had a chance to say goodbye. I know he would have looked at me and said, "Mom, I love you more than anything." I can feel the familiar longing for just one more conversation with him running through my body, and my anxiety shoots into high gear.

Another panic attack kicks in. My breathing is harsh, and the lights on the bar used in the treatment are flashing. I'm sobbing hard and grab the wastebasket again, but only bile comes up. I gag while the tears run down my face. My nose is dripping, and my hair is wet and sticking to my face. My therapist is trying to calm me down and bring me to the present, but I'm not coming back. In fact, I want to stay where I am. I wish I could die on his couch with my head buried in the wastebasket. He encourages me to try and move through it, gently reminding me that I'm not actually there. He tells me I'm watching it as if it's on a screen, but it feels so real.

Next, I see Shaun's spirit start to leave his body, and he reaches out to me. I grab his hand and hold on with all my might. I know he wants me to save him, and more than I need my next breath, I want to keep him here, but I can't . . . his fingers are slipping right through mine. As hard as I try to hold on, I'm losing my grip. His physical hand transforms into a transparent, gleaming white spiritual hand even though the rest of his soul is still connected to his physical form. He's letting go, and there's nothing I can do to stop it. I hold on as tightly as I can, but his hand pulls free, and he floats away, out of my reach.

The terror that sweeps through me is agonizing. I don't know how to live without him; he was such a light in my world. Will he wait for me? I'm afraid when I get to heaven, he may be in a higher place reserved for the best. I think he was a better person than I, and he may be closer to God than I could ever be. I pray I'll be allowed to be with him. I need to know his spirit will stay near me every moment of the day and, most of all, that he'll wait for me. There's a song called "Save a Place for Me" by Matthew West that says what I feel. Oh, please, God, let him save a place for me.

If I had died, I think Shaun would have been more patient with this thing called death. He was so strong and positive; he would have handled it better. But not me—I don't want to wait to be reunited. I want it now. I want to laugh with him as we did before. Not later. Now! The unfairness of it all fills me with rage.

My therapist's voice brings me back to the present. I try to stand up, but my legs buckle. I can't hold myself up. At the start of the session, my hands were pressed to my heart. Now, they're clenching my throat—it feels as if the trauma is trying to claw its way out of my body. I can't believe the level of exhaustion I feel. How can I go through another session like this, much less a series of them? When I leave, I'm certain I'll never return.

The next day, my therapist calls to check on me. I tell him there's no way I can walk through that door again. The reliving of the memories and images of that day sent me into a tailspin—I can't bear the thought of going any deeper into the details of Shaun's death.

My therapist is understanding but persistent. He says that my PTSD (post-traumatic stress disorder) on a scale of one to ten, is currently at level nine. He tells me if I stick it out, he can get me to a four. After years of trying to keep everything at bay, the thought of deliberately dragging them out and reliving the most traumatic events of my life sends jolts of fear through me. But the idea of cutting my fear and anxiety in half makes me reconsider. I want my life back. I agree to schedule the next session, but I'm not sure I'll be able to keep the appointment. I hang up the phone, close my eyes, and say a prayer that I just might stand a chance.

CHAPTER TWO

THE EARLY YEARS

While we try to teach our children all about life,
our children teach us what life is all about.
—Angela Schwindt

I GREW UP a mile from a small rural town in Wisconsin that had a population under three hundred, even during the baby boom. My parents raised me in a Christian home. My mother, Lorraine, came from a large family and was a devout Catholic. My father, Harold, was a Methodist. My parents were from the same town of Kennan, Wisconsin, but they met while working in Milwaukee. They taught me to be fair, to be honest, to work hard in life, and not to gossip or talk ill of anybody. We had to attend church every Sunday and CCD (religious education) in a class on Wednesdays. It was more than an expectation—it was a requirement. There was never a good excuse to miss Mass or CCD. I was given a solid Christian foundation, for which I'm grateful.

I was the eldest of three sisters and a brother. We were a close family and lived under the simple values of farming life. My parents had an agricultural lime hauling business and a farm. During the spring, summer, and fall my father spent many long hours spreading lime on fields throughout Northern Wisconsin. My parents and most of us kids spent hours doing chores in the barn. While my dad was working all day in the fields, my mother had her hands full taking care of her kids. Having five children in seven years was chaotic. We had different personalities and describing them all would take another book! My mother was our hair stylist and seamstress. She made sure our hair was cut, and she liked to perm mine. Through the years, I had overly tight perms until she figured out the proper technique. Mom spent her life and a couple of sewing machines making everything for us, including my first prom dress. Her days were full of doing chores, taking care of us kids, cooking, baking, grooming us, and sewing.

The work ethic of my parents was instilled in us at a young age. They both taught me how to work hard and not give up. Little did I know this not-give-up attitude would get tested many times throughout my life, but never could I have imagined I would have to go through losing a child.

Every week my grandma came over, and Mom would wash and style her hair. She always brought us a bag of cookies, and we loved spending time with her. I was the first grandchild to be born to one of my grandparents' ten children. Along with my aunts and uncles, they spoiled me. In time, the rest of the family followed God's plan to "be fruitful and multiply," and they had an orchard of grandchildren, but I always held a special place in Grandma's heart.

I spent a lot of time during the summer visiting my grandparent's farm, which left me with beautiful memories. My days were spent with the animals—puppies and kittens, bunnies, horses, even a duck that followed me around at the lake. I had adventures and excitement. I often brought a new pet home, which drove my mother crazy. She would say, "I can't wait until you have your own place, and you can have all the animals you want."

As I grew older, so did my love of animals, especially the horses. I saddled up my horse to ride every day. I never felt more alive than when I was galloping across the farmland or down a logging trail with the wind in my face and the open sky above me. Over time, many more horses came into my life. I always found my dad's soft spot and convinced him to get just one more. I spent one summer peeling poplar until my fingers were raw so I could build a training corral for my horses. Each one held a special place in my heart, but Black Satin was my favorite.

Life on the farm was innocent and fun—a child's paradise. We worked hard but we played hard as well. Several neighborhood kids and my sisters and brother played softball in the field behind our house until dark. On a hot summer day, we would convince Mom to take us to our favorite lake.

My brother and I went to a nearby creek to catch tadpoles. During the winter, we gathered the neighbors, grabbed our sleds, and would slide down a nearby hill. I couldn't decide if I liked summer or winter best. As long as I was outside, I was happy.

I lurched into my teens and wanted to earn money to buy a car, so I picked up odd jobs like cleaning sod from the sidewalks in town, mowing lawns, and scrubbing down my uncle's work truck. Uncle Dan worked in masonry construction, and his heavy-duty pickup was a nightmare every time I cleaned it. When I was 14, my parents decided it was time to go from one bathroom to two, and they remodeled the house. My brother was elated—he'd shared it with his sisters long enough.

The remodeling brought more than a new bathroom into our lives, though . . . I fell in love with one of the builders, Fran. He was a good-looking, athletic guy who was in college and studying to be a physical education teacher. He was older than me, and all the other girls were jealous. In the town where I grew up, if you went to college, it was a big deal. I saw an exciting future with him, but my parents were not impressed. They saw me getting involved with a much older guy and didn't want me to miss out on the freedom of my teenage years. But young love prevailed over our parents' wishes.

Like every teenage girl with stars in her eyes, I had lofty dreams about how my life with Fran would be. I daydreamed about us exploring the world outside of our little Midwest town. We'd move to a real city, find a cozy apartment, and I would go to college too, perhaps studying interior design or business—I wasn't sure yet. First, however, I needed to finish high school, and Fran promised he would wait for me. This was quite a commitment for him since I had three years left until I finished! As a result, my high school years weren't spent the way other kids spent theirs. My friends hung out together and dated different people, exploring their options and life in general, while I stayed focused on my boyfriend. Later on, I saw that I missed out on having important experiences in the most formative years of my life.

My vision of our future crumbled when a couple of months before we got married, Fran's dad took a job in upper Michigan and told us he wanted us to stay in our hometown and take over the family farm. I'd loved spending my childhood years at my grandparents' place, but I'd seen firsthand what a hard life farming is. I'd watched them struggle to make ends meet, and I knew I didn't want that life. I was also disappointed that my dream of college would have to be put on hold or maybe forgotten altogether. But Fran had to help his parents—it was his duty. He was convinced that the farm would provide a good life for us, and he assured me that he'd take on the brunt of the heavy lifting. Although it wasn't what I'd planned for my life, I got swept up by his rush of excitement. The romanticism of working together under the summer sun won me over, and I agreed.

My parents tried talking us out of it, but how could I not marry Fran when he'd waited so long for me? At seventeen, just two weeks after I graduated high school, I walked down the aisle on my father's arm. I was afraid, but I lacked the courage to back out. I convinced myself everything would work out fine—after all, most people where I grew up got married right out of high school and started a family. Why should I be different?

We settled into our new life, and I figured out what it meant to be a farmer's wife pretty fast. It wasn't glamorous, but I told myself it would be enough. My horses were my saving grace. By moving to the farm, I didn't have to give them up, and they kept me company during the lonely days. The farm was rural and isolated, but I developed a strong connection with our neighbors, Sue and Lynn, who helped me feel I wasn't alone. Fran quit college and said goodbye to his dream of becoming a P.E. teacher. He worked hard to keep the farm going and stuck to his promise that he'd do most of the heavy work, but I couldn't sit on the sidelines and watch. Soon, I was in the thick of it. I learned how to milk cows, drive the tractor, sow crops, and everything else that had to be done to keep the farm alive. We both worked long, exhausting days. It wasn't the life I'd planned on, but it was my reality. Despite all our hard work, it was sometimes hard to scrape enough money together to put food on the table. We relied on our garden a lot, and I carried credit at the grocery store. At times, we had to ask for financial help from our families.

We were married a year when I got pregnant with my first child. We were so excited to be having a baby, but I was scared too. I was so young and petite, and the doctor said I could never deliver a baby over six pounds. When I was four months along, I woke up to use the bathroom— a nightly ritual during my pregnancy. It was always an annoyance, but this time it was a blessing. I was going back to bed and heard a crackling noise in the walls. I thought it was the cold outside causing the house to make popping sounds, but something didn't feel right. It alarmed me enough to wake my husband.

Our bedroom was on the main floor, and the staircase was in our room.

Fran went downstairs and checked the wood stove we used during winter to save on our heating costs. Everything seemed fine so he came back to bed and went to sleep, but I lay awake listening. I was alarmed and sensed something was wrong. The crackling was closer.

I woke him again. "Listen, it's getting louder. It sounds as if it's coming from upstairs."

Fran dashed up the steps and opened the door at the top. Smoke billowed out and filled the stairwell. He shut the door to block it and yelled, "Call the fire department."

I reached for the phone but there was no dial tone—the fire had destroyed the lines. Throwing on an oversized t-shirt, sweatpants, and my work boots, I ran to the barn to use the phone there to call the fire department. We still had a connection, but I was so panicked, I couldn't find the number. I called my mom instead and asked her to contact the fire department. She started crying as I described what was happening—she knew from experience how devastating this was going to be for us.

Unfortunately, we'd been through a fire before in our family. When I was little, we got a similar phone call telling us that my grandparents' barn was on fire. Their house was five miles away, and when we walked out of our house, we could see the amber glow off in the sky on the horizon. My parents helped get the animals out of the barn while we kids watched from afar, wondering if our favorite kittens would be okay. The next day, we went over to visit Grandma and Grandpa and couldn't believe our eyes—the barn we loved to play in was gone. My tabby kitten never did come back. It took years to get the image of the barn burning out of my head. Now, I couldn't believe I was out in the snow watching my home burn. My whole life was going up in smoke.

I hung up with my mother, and while running back to the house to help my husband, I fell on my back in a patch of slippery ice. Pain shot through my body, and I grabbed my stomach. *I can't lose this baby*, I thought. When I struggled back to my feet, I saw flames so high they reached the top of the pine trees. Burning branches broke away and toppled through the roof of the house. Although I was dizzy from the fall, I dashed into the house to help save what we could. The first thing I saw was my plant stand in the living room. Without thinking, I carried the stand with all the plants still on it and sat it in the middle of the yard. It was a crazy thing to do—within minutes, my plants were stiff with ice.

I rushed back in and grabbed the toaster and electric frying pan. Fran took the stereo, but he forgot it was still connected to the wall. Hearing sirens, he realized he was in his underwear and ran back inside to grab his pants. We were overjoyed to see the fire trucks pull up, but then they discovered their pump was frozen solid due to the extreme cold. Once they saw the house couldn't be saved, the firemen tried to break into a back bedroom to retrieve our wedding gifts. We had been storing them in there, unused, saving them for the future: our best dishes, fancy platters, pretty towels, and handmade blankets. Our clothes were kept in that bedroom too.

The fire was so hot, however, that glass was blowing out of the windows, preventing anybody from getting any closer. We all stood back and watched the home that my husband and his family had grown up in crumble to the ground. Neither of us could wrap our heads around what had happened. One minute we were warm in our beds and the next we were shivering outside in the sub-zero night. Within a few hours, our home and all our belongings were a pile of ashes.

The sun rose and the chores had to be done . . . cows didn't care about our loss. At least I already had the right clothes on—my work clothes and boots were all I had left to wear. We literally had nothing but the clothes on our backs. Fran went to the field to round up the cows. There were always a few strays that he had to scout for, so while he did that, I would use the pitchfork to fill the wheelbarrows with corn silage.

This morning, though, my back hurt too much from falling on the ice to handle the job. Fran did it all while I fed the calves and did what little I could. We fed one large wheelbarrow to every two cows, so there were more than twenty to fill. Our farm was not modernized, but we had stopped milking our cows by hand. We'd wash their udders and carry the milker from one cow to the next, dumping the milk after each cow. The process took two hours when we worked together, but this morning we had to allow for my back injury and our shared tears, so it took longer. Even on the best days, this wasn't an easy job, and today we were beyond exhausted.

We went through the motions of our chores in a daze before returning to the house to see if there was anything left to salvage, but the ashes were still smoldering. It would be days before they were cool enough for us to look through them. The only things standing were the wood stove and the chimney, which were still burning. As I stood there trying to comprehend the damage, a sharp jab in my back brought me back to reality. I could feel

I was spotting, and a wave of terror swept over me—were we going to lose our child as well as our home? I began to pray to God, begging to be spared this pain. The doctor put me on complete bed rest, so we went to my parents' house, where I rested for several days until the bleeding stopped. I knew God was beside me; we'd made it through.

Finally, the ashes cooled enough for us to enter them. We kicked through them wearing our heavy boots, hoping to find something we could keep. At first, the only things that turned up were broken pieces of dishes and bits of glass. I was just about to walk away when a ray of sunlight caught a glint of gold. I reached into the ashes and to my amazement, pulled out my confirmation cross. The heat had distorted it, but it was still my gold cross, unblemished at that. Once again, I felt God's presence surrounding me.

CHAPTER THREE

BECOMING A MOTHER

What a gift God has given me in this child.
I will cherish it always.
—Cindy Baumann

IT WAS ONLY logical that we move in with my parents while we figured out what to do next. We'd been renting the house from Fran's parents, and they didn't have a lot of insurance over the place. It would take weeks to process the claim, and in the end, they lost far more than was paid out. We were depressed over the situation, but the excitement of expecting our baby helped us get through the months ahead. Every morning and night, Fran and I traveled to the farm to do our chores. It was a grueling schedule, but time passed quickly and before we knew it, we were heading to the hospital to welcome our first child.

After a long labor, our son Ryan came into the world. I was very lucky to avoid a Cesarean. He was a very big baby, and they had to X-ray me to see if he could make it through the birth canal. In the end, forceps were necessary. What a beautiful boy he was, with a perfect head of brown hair that later turned almost white, and sweet brown eyes which were stunning against his light hair. My world revolved around him, and life was good again.

Living with my parents and four siblings was chaotic; however, my younger sister Cheryl was a tremendous help to me when Ryan was born. She was really like a second mother to him. When Ryan was three weeks old, he started vomiting violently with such force that the milk would shoot out of his mouth and land several feet away. We took him to the pediatrician, and he was diagnosed with pyloric stenosis, a condition his father had as a baby. It is an uncommon hereditary condition in infants that blocks food from entering the small intestine. There is a muscular valve between the stomach and intestine that holds food in the stomach until it's ready for the next stage in the digestive process. It was this muscle that blocked the food. The thought of our baby having surgery was so frightening, but Ryan was tough and breezed through it. He looked at me as if to ask what all the fuss was about—and then he smiled for the first time. I was so relieved that he was better, but now we had medical bills on top of the financial strain of the farm.

Because of the number of people living in my parents' house, it was difficult for everybody. Tempers were frayed, and Fran, Ryan, and I needed our own space—we knew we had to make a change. The only thing standing was the barn, and we couldn't move in with the cows, so while we waited for the house to be rebuilt, we borrowed a small camper from a friend. There was one bedroom, a tiny area for the kitchen, and a small space where the crib sat. Our water came from a garden hose that we ran from the barn. There was no bathroom, so we had to improvise. We bought a portable potty, and that was our toilet for the next six months. I didn't mind using the portable potty, but I hated dumping it! We roughed it in the camper until the house was done, no easy task with an energetic baby in the midst of it all. On top of this, we had a barn full of cows that had to be cared for, and they needed milking morning and night. We had crops to plant and harvest, and my spoiled horses demanded attention.

Clearly, we needed to figure out a way to build a house on the property, but we didn't think we'd be approved for a loan. It was with trepidation that we visited a local bank. Fran's parents gave us what they could to help out, and to our great relief and gratitude, the bank agreed to work with us to cover the balance. The months went by as Fran labored to build our home. He had spent summers working with his grandpa, who was a meticulous carpenter, so he learned from the best. I knew our house would be well-built, and it had the bonus of being ours. I was so excited to see it going up. Fran hired his cousin and a neighbor to help him, and by fall our house was finished.

It was a happy day when we got out of the camper and into our home. By then, Ryan was crawling, so the timing was perfect. And yet, as I laid my head on the pillow that first night in our new home, I couldn't find peace. I woke in the night and swore I heard the crackling sound of fire. I had to get up and walk through every room in the house to make sure it was okay. Those fears and the resulting nightmares stayed with me for years. The unhealed fear that I carried deep inside me was one of the first layers of trauma in my life. That's when I learned to start pushing my fears into that hidden box in the closet of my mind.

I wanted to earn money for our family and decided to put my hobbies to use. I'd always been creative, so I taught myself how to make silk flower arrangements, wreaths, Christmas ornaments, and all kinds of fun crafts that I sold at a nursing home several miles away. I also took a job waitressing to bring in extra cash, and it felt like we were on the road to recovery. Soon after, however, I got the stomach flu, and as the weeks passed, it didn't go away. I finally went to the doctor to see what was wrong. The doctor ran some tests and said, "Cindy, this is going to be the longest flu in history—you're pregnant again, my dear."

I can laugh about it now, but my mom told me that I couldn't get pregnant while I was nursing—boy, did we lay that old wives' tale to rest! Ryan was just six months old, and I was pregnant with my next son. With our financial situation at the time, it was the last thing we needed. As the crippling morning sickness subsided, the pregnancy went well. I continued to help in the barn and put crops in alongside my husband. One day under the summer sun, I drove the tractor in extreme heat. It was hay season in Wisconsin, and there wasn't a choice—the hay had to be brought in before the rains came.

That night, I ran a high fever and became delirious. My mom came over and put ice packs on my head, begging me to quit working on the farm. I was eight months pregnant, and she was concerned about my safety as well as the baby's. I did what she said and stayed out of the sun and rested. Slowly, I gained my strength back.

My due date came and went. Finally, I went into labor—ten days overdue. This time, things moved fast, and soon the contractions were three minutes apart. We dropped Ryan off at a neighbor's and set off on the forty-five-minute trip to the hospital. As we walked in the door, I had no choice but to squat, and the nurses pulled me down the hall. They yelled, "You can't sit! You're close to having this baby." They put me into a delivery room, but it still took some time before Shaun was born. This time, I had excessive bleeding. They gave me several shots, packed me with gauze, unpacked me, and packed me again.

When it was all over, the doctor came in and said, "You are done—never again. Your babies are too big, and your body is too small to handle it." When they put that eight-pound, nine-ounce, adorable baby boy in my arms, the world stood still. I named him Shaun and couldn't have loved him more. I was complete, and a wave of contentment washed over me.

The next few months were busy with a newborn and a fifteen-month-old. The boys brought happiness to my life, but they took every ounce of energy I had to keep up with them and still help with the farm. Shaun was a happy baby, a beautiful gift to us all. He was growing like crazy, and his older brother Ryan was in awe of this new little presence in our lives. I envisioned them being best friends.

Then, when he was three months old, my mom looked into his eyes and said, "Cindy, I think you should call the doctor. His pupils are different sizes. There's something wrong."

I called immediately, and they told me to bring him in. They said it was probably Horner's syndrome, which can be caused by a severe ear infection . . . but Shaun had never had an ear infection. "Maybe you weren't aware he had one," the doctor said. I was sure I'd have known if my baby had been ill, but I hoped they were right.

They checked for fluid on his brain and found it to be normal. Next, they referred us to Marshfield Clinic and St. Joseph's Hospital, a larger health care system located in Marshfield, Wisconsin, where more serious conditions and diseases are treated. I knew this meant they were searching for something bad, and I was scared—what could be wrong with my baby? They took some X-rays and admitted him into the hospital. That evening, the doctor said they'd found a growth in his chest. I asked if they could remove it, but he said they wouldn't know until they did more tests. The next couple of weeks were filled with spinal taps, bone scans, CT scans, kidney scans, biopsies, and more. It wasn't until they did a bone marrow biopsy that I put everything together.

"When I hear bone marrow, I think of cancer."

The doctor's answer was chilling: "We are anticipating this to be a malignant tumor, yes."

I slumped to the floor in shock. Sobbing, I crawled to the crib to grab my baby. As I hugged him, it seemed impossible that I'd just heard the word *cancer*. I was twenty-one years old and had never heard of a child getting cancer. The only people I'd heard of with cancer were adults, and they'd all died.

They suspected Shaun had neuroblastoma, a rare childhood cancer. It develops from nerve cells in the fetus called neuroblasts. In a healthy child, the neuroblasts develop normally. In very rare cases, they are cancerous and cause neuroblastoma, which grows in the form of a tumor. In the United States, eight hundred children are diagnosed with this cancer every year. The odds are low, but it was our turn. I couldn't help but wonder if I'd done something to cause it. I thought about the day I came in from the fields with a high temperature while I was pregnant. Did that cause it? The doctor reassured me that it was just bad luck, and it was nothing I'd done, but I was searching for a reason. That night, we closed our eyes on day one of the first of many battles.

The doctors alerted us to all the risks of surgery, including possible paralysis due to the location of the tumor, but we had no option but to go forward with it. I'll never forget the day I had to hand my son over to the doctors and watch him go into the operating room without me. They opened his chest to remove the growth, which left an incision that went halfway around his body. Their original diagnosis was confirmed: our baby had neuroblastoma. All we could do was cry and hold him as he healed.

Shaun became part of a research group with a team of doctors around the world. We were then told that treating him with radiation to his chest would give him a cure rate of 98 percent. They were going to put live radiation into my tiny baby. He couldn't even support his head yet—and they called that treatment? Radiation therapy carried its own set of risks. The most serious ones were the possibility of developing thyroid cancer or terminal bone cancer. After they explained all this, they left us alone to decide whether to sign the papers or not. They were only doing us lip service, though—they knew it was his best chance. There was no other choice.

Shaun wasn't cured by radiation alone. When he was nine months old, the nightmare singled us out again. They found another mass on the right side of his neck, and he was scheduled for his second surgery. The tumor had massed several lymph nodes together and was growing around his jugular vein. It had also attached to the base of his brain. After hours of surgery, the surgeon explained that it was inoperable. There was no choice but to start chemotherapy on my tiny baby. They had to shrink the tumor before they could remove it. He was admitted to the hospital and given treatments for five days consecutively every three weeks, administered through intravenous injections.

The treatments were so hard on Shaun. On the first day of each chemo cycle, he would vomit every fifteen minutes. His chemotherapy treatments were difficult to administer too. He would often go through several IVs because either the vein collapsed or the IV infiltrated. One of the drugs was so toxic that if he moved and the drug got into his system, it would burn the tissue in his arm and skin grafting would be necessary, so he had to be sedated first. When he was sick from the chemotherapy, I would crawl in the crib with him and soothe him enough for him to sleep. I rarely left his side, and our bond became unshakable.

There were times that his white blood cell count dropped so low we could lose him at any moment. A normal count ranges from 5,000 to 10,000, but after a particular treatment, he developed a bronchial infection with a WBC count of only 500. He had hardly any white blood cells to fight infection. The doctors were concerned that he would develop pneumonia and be too weak to survive it. I had to take him in every day to have his blood counts checked. They kept him on antibiotics as a precaution. All the nurses who cared for him fell in love with the sweet little boy who fought his illness with such grace.

Everybody was amazed when after eight months of chemotherapy, he pulled through for the second time. When he was 18 months old, the doctors said the tumor was small enough for a third surgery. This time, we were looking at even more extreme complications: possible paralysis of the right side of his body and loss of nerve function to his face, tongue, and shoulder—if he even came through it. For the third time, we had no choice. The operation had to be done; all we could do was hope for the best.

This time, the surgeon opened the right side of Shaun's neck and performed a radical right neck procedure, which included the removal of muscles, lymph nodes, tissue, and blood vessels within the neck and down to his shoulder, leaving only the main artery to the brain. The complex operation took eight hours. Our skilled surgeon successfully removed almost all the tumor but had to leave a portion near the base of the brain that was impossible to detach. Shaun was moved to recovery and then intensive care.

With some of the malignant tumor left inside my son's body, there was another important decision to make, and it could significantly impact

Shaun's future. We had to choose between radiation therapy to his neck, brain, and spine or continuing with chemotherapy. Shaun's doctor reached out to the other specialists in the research group, and after several conferences and consultations, they suggested we continue with chemotherapy rather than radiation. The strength of radiation in all those areas could cripple Shaun and cause facial disfiguration. They didn't want to leave him scarred if they could avoid it. They believed he had a good chance of survival and they wanted him to enjoy his life.

Considering what that baby had just endured, Shaun did remarkably well, but for the next three years, we lived every day in fear of him getting sick without having any immunity to protect him. We had to shelter him until he was finished with treatment and his immune system had time to recoup. He wasn't a normal little kid with a normal life. We couldn't take him anywhere, and we were afraid to venture out ourselves in case we brought something home to him. We had to protect him from the world and everything in it. There were no playdates or going to church as a family. We couldn't even make a quick trip to the grocery store. Anything that involved people was off-limits. His immune system was so compromised that a simple cold could turn into pneumonia and kill him, and if he were to contract chicken pox, it would be unthinkable.

A difficult stage for us to deal with was when he lost his hair. He had a beautiful head of almost-white hair that shimmered over his bright icy-blue eyes. The loss of his beautiful hair was the most recognizable and visible label that he was a child with cancer. He'd already been through so much—and now, when we looked at him, we saw how much the life-saving treatment was costing him. On one occasion, he was lying on the couch and when he got up, he saw his hair all over the seat.

He said, "Mom, please put it back on. I want hair like you."

He loved me to comb and blow-dry his hair after a bath and when it fell out, it was hard for him. Every night when Shaun said his prayers, he would ask Jesus to heal his "owie." It was devastating for us to put him through so much misery. How do you explain to a child that another doctor visit is going to help him when all he wants to do is be well enough to play like everybody else?

His fourth surgery was done at the age of two, and we received good news: the surgeon removed five swollen lymph nodes and the results were all negative. They would continue chemotherapy for another six months in the hope of killing the remaining cancer cells at the base of his brain.

Every time his poor little body was wracked in pain., I prayed the cancer would finally be eradicated.

Fran and I suffered greatly over Shaun's illness, but it affected the extended family too. Everybody helped where they could, but sometimes they were too busy with their own lives to be with us. Fran often had to be home to take care of the farm while I was in the hospital. At those times, it was just Shaun and me. I sat through one surgery by myself, spending the hours in prayer that he would make it through. I was so afraid he would die. After all the years of treatment he'd gone through, I couldn't bear the thought of having to give my baby boy back to God.

I was also very worried about Ryan's emotional state. It was horrible for me leaving one child behind and watching the other one suffer so much. Ryan loved his grandma, but he missed his family where he had been the center of attention for fifteen months. Now, he had to share the attention with his sick brother and had to give up the life he had known at home with his mom, dad, and brother. He felt abandoned and he rejected me when I came home. He wanted Grandma, and it broke my heart, even though I understood. My sister Cheryl was there again to give Ryan extra love and care.

After four years, the treatments ended, and it was officially declared that Shaun was in remission. The odds were slim, but he'd beaten them. The doctors would monitor him with frequent visits for the rest of his childhood. After spending so much of the last four years sleeping in the hospital with him, I expected relief, but a new fear set in. Without treatment keeping cancer away, would it come back? I prayed to God to please let me keep my baby.

One night after I cried myself to sleep, I was awakened in the middle of the night by a beautiful presence in my room. It was dark, with just a glimmer of the moon shining through the window. I couldn't see anybody, and I didn't hear them speak, but a message was passed on to me saying, "Shaun is going to be okay." I was alert from the second I opened my eyes, listening, as the telepathic voice repeated, "He is going to be okay." The presence of God filled the room that night, and his message of hope gave me a sense of calmness I hadn't had in years. The presence was larger than life and yet so intimate, I felt surrounded by love and protection. In that moment, I finally let myself believe that my son would survive. I knew it was a visit from God to bring comfort to my life—and it did.

CHAPTER FOUR

RE-INVENTING MYSELF

*Never be afraid to fall apart because it is an opportunity
to rebuild yourself the way you wish you had been all along.*
—Rae Smith

KNOWING SHAUN WAS free of cancer brought us joy and relief,
but the trauma we went through took its toll on our marriage. For so long,
Fran and I had lived with the terror of losing our son. The experience had
pushed us apart. While I'd been desperate for a hug and reassurance that
Shaun would make it, my husband had closed me out, dealing with his
sadness privately. He was carrying a huge weight of repressed anger which
led him to verbally mistreat me. He swore at me, called me stupid, and said
some mean things over the years. This diminished my self-confidence and
devalued me. I felt dumb.

I now understand where his anger came from. He was harboring a
secret only the two of us knew. The secret took me a long time to adjust
to. When he was nineteen, his first girlfriend got pregnant at sixteen. She
wanted an abortion and he supported her decision, but afterwards he
carried tremendous guilt. He also struggled with many family disputes,
which was hard on him. Since I was the one closest to him, I was an easy
target. His inner torment spilled over to me.

Between work, the financial pressure of farming, and Shaun's illness, our fragile marriage began to crumble. We needed professional help to guide us through the anguish that comes with caring for a child with cancer, but we were too busy just surviving and keeping our child alive to take time for anything else. We were young ourselves and ill-equipped for what we were facing. We had no idea how to live and love while dealing with a very sick child.

I would be in the hospital for a week and home for two, then gone again. There was no structure in our home or time for loving each other and enjoying the simple things a young family should enjoy. We never took time for one another and didn't know how to anymore. We didn't even know how to love or comfort ourselves. Our minds were constantly on the pressures of keeping Shaun alive and having enough money to buy food. Each day was like living on a battlefield, and we were both trying to avoid the land mines of life.

My heart was breaking, and I yearned for comfort and to feel worthy and loved, but I felt anything but. I was broken, worn down, and tired. I wanted out, but our families wouldn't hear of it. Divorce wasn't an option—it wasn't what you did. We lived in the house together, but our hearts weren't connected. Just when we started to recover from one blow, it seemed like the next one hit us. We were hurting and couldn't heal from all we had been through. This wasn't the life we envisioned, and it was getting harder to make the best of it. We were both drowning under the stress and pressure of it all.

Neither of us had any idea how to manage the emotions we felt. I cried all the time, while Fran tried to be strong and shut me out. When he wasn't stacking hay bales in the barn, he would take long walks in the woods or play softball to release some stress, and I would sit alone and cry. Looking back, I wish we had been offered professional counseling through the hospital to help us communicate the pain we were going through. We were both at fault and I certainly take responsibility for what happened to us.

The impact of a teen marriage, the illness of our baby, and the pressures of the farm were intolerable. We just couldn't find our way out of the whirlpool of hurt and anger we created. Finally, I reached a point where I couldn't turn back. I wanted to break free from this life full of tragedy, hurt, and disappointment, and at last set out to follow my dreams. I kept wondering what was outside of my little world. Interior design and business still intrigued me, and I believed if I could go to college, meet new people, and have fun, life on the other side of this heartache would be better. I realized that when I married Fran at seventeen, I had no idea what lay ahead. We couldn't have foreseen what was to come. I had to face the fact that I was too young to navigate the obstacles we'd been battered by.

Fran knew it too. We'd reached an impasse and had to face the process of a painful and complicated divorce. We loved the boys with all our hearts, and that was the only thing left for us to fight about. We were both good parents, and we fought for custody. The battle was ugly, and I cried as I watched my young love turn so hateful in front of family and strangers. If I could turn back time and take away the sadness and confusion my children experienced through our divorce, I would. I live with deep regret about that period in our lives.

The day I left Fran, our farm, and the familiarity of my hometown was unbearable. I'd put some basic belongings into a trailer, secured my two little boys in the backseat, and set out for my new home, an apartment two hours away in Wausau, Wisconsin. I will never forget the look on his face or my boys' as we separated. I could see he was afraid and angry at the world. The love was gone between us, and the air was thick with hurt and loss. The boys had to move out of their home to a new city where we didn't know anybody, and this wouldn't be their last move. I was selfish and thought the kids would be resilient. I was too young to understand the ramifications. Ryan was only six when his innocent childhood was taken away. He was quiet and withdrawn, and just wanted his family back together. Shaun, who was five, seemed to weather the storm better, at least on the surface. I told them I was sorry, and that everything would be okay, but the guilt inside was eating me alive. I told them, "Your dad and I can't live together anymore, but we both love you very much," but of course that made no sense to them.

We lived at the end of a dirt road, and when I reached the blacktop county road, headed for an unknown future, I stopped the car, cupped my hands over my eyes, and cried. I almost turned around, but I told myself it was too late. We had been through too much; we'd forgotten what it was like to laugh and to have dreams. We needed the opportunity to start over . . . to feel young again. For seven years, other than a few glimmers of happiness around the birth of our boys, sadness and tears had filled my life. I could see no other way than to have a fresh start. I prayed that God would give Fran, the children, and me a second chance at happiness.

An added pain was separation from my precious horses. They had been my saving grace over the years, but now because I had nowhere to keep them, I had to say goodbye to them. I cried all the way to our small apartment. My tears blurred my vision, and it was only with God's guidance that we got there safely. When I got to the city that I had always dreamed about, I was afraid. A good friend of mine, Deenah, who was from my hometown and had previously helped out with my boys, moved in with us. We had a nice friendship and a great time together, and she loved my kids. Having a friendly face around made adjusting much easier and more fun. As time went by, I branched out and explored my world. I made new girlfriends and even dated some interesting guys. My children enjoyed Deenah living with us, and the companionship was nice. It felt good to be young and free from the struggle of my marriage. I tried things I'd never done—I went downhill skiing and signed up for a volleyball team. I felt joy burning in my heart again.

Fran and I had the kids on alternate weekends, and whenever the boys were with me, I made sure it was all about them. Ryan was hesitant to try new things, but when he did, he was a natural, so we signed up for roller-skating lessons and learned to downhill ski at the mountain near our home. Shaun was eager to try everything, especially if it meant he got to be outside. The boys had playdates with other children at the McDonald's playground, and we spent wonderful days on Rib Mountain, looking down at the beautiful new city that belonged to us. I cherish the memories we made together at that time. Seeing them smile as they explored new things was the best healing for us all. There were always a few days of adjustment when the boys came back from their father, and I could sense a little coldness toward me. I knew in their hearts, they wanted their mom and dad back together.

I tried to be a good mother to my boys, but my heart hurt for breaking up our family. I was the one who walked out, and I lived with that reality every day. I felt selfish, but it did no good wallowing in guilt. I put one foot ahead of the other, trying to build a better life for myself and my children. That year, I reached a milestone and fulfilled one of my biggest dreams—I enrolled in college. My advisor read that I wanted to go into computer programing, which sounded like a lucrative field with great job opportunities. The college didn't offer interior design and I thought this was the best fit. My advisor had the foresight to ask if I was sure it was the best field for me. I thought for a moment and had to answer with an honest, "No."

"Based on your personality and what you like to do, I feel marketing would be a great fit for you," he said.

He was right, and I'm so glad I took his advice. Even though I was working full-time as a temporary secretary and made a little over minimum wage, I entered college and studied at night. At work, I was filling in for a woman on maternity leave and knew I'd have to find another job in the middle of my semester.

Fate stepped in to help me, and after the secretary returned, my manager told me they wanted to keep me on but wanted to move me into sales and marketing. I proved myself in that role, and soon I was sought by a popular local radio station. I was so excited when they offered me a good base pay plus commission on any sales I brought in. This was my big chance, and I took the plunge. I loved my job and was a quick learner. In no time, I was making more money than I had ever dreamed of—which still wasn't a lot. The kids were impressed that I was part of a large radio station, as there was some prestige attached to working there. We attended events, met celebrities, and the boys got to ride on the company float in the Christmas parade. It was very exciting to them since they'd grown up in such a rural area and missed out on a lot of social activities because of Shaun's illness. It felt good to prove to my parents, siblings, and former husband that I wasn't a failure.

Up to this point in my life, I didn't know what it was like to make more than minimum wage. In my excitement, I bragged about my job too much, and one day a family member said something to put me in my place: "You sure talk a lot about how much money you make. We have heard it all before." Ouch. That hurt, but she was right. I took a good look at myself and saw at the root of my pride was the desire to prove to everybody that I wasn't a failure. Most of all, I wanted to prove it to myself. That moment of insight was a major step in the process of rebuilding my sense of worth and confidence.

Shortly after my success at the radio station, a local CBS television station approached me and offered me an even better package, providing another step in my career. These advancements made me feel better about myself, but they also taught me that no amount of success could relieve guilt, and it certainly couldn't replace love. Despite what I achieved, my heart was empty. I beat myself up over my decision to leave Fran, largely because of the hurt I had caused the boys but out of concern for Fran as well. He'd suffered a loss of self-esteem, just as I had. He felt he'd failed by not completing college, by selling the cows, and because our marriage ended. The guilt of terminating the pregnancy with his girlfriend still haunted him. He was under tremendous pressure at the farm since our divorce. He was running things on his own, and it put so much financial responsibility on his shoulders. He believed that God was punishing him.

When the company his father worked for in Michigan offered him a position as foreman at a plant in Idaho, Fran took the job. He was ready for his fresh start, and I think he wanted to prove to me he could do it. He knew being so far away would be hard on the boys, but it was time to make his way in the world. I let the kids go to Idaho to be with Fran during the summer months. He was a good father, and it was only fair; however, it broke my heart to put the boys on a plane and send them away for such a long time. After the first long season apart, I considered the pain we were going through and decided to give my marriage another try. I wanted to believe we could make it together, now that we had matured and learned more about life.

I resigned from my position at the television station and moved to Idaho to live with Fran. We were determined to make a go of it, but it didn't take long to realize that although things had changed outwardly, the inner issues were still the same. The hurt between us ran too deep, and the move had just added one more brick in the wall. I wanted things to be better for the kids, but they weren't. It wasn't fair for the boys to see us fighting. There was too much past hurt between us to start over. That ship had sailed, and I should have left it out to sea. I could see the hurt in my little boys' faces and yet, I felt it was better for them to be surrounded by real love. Even if they didn't understand, I thought leaving was best for everybody.

Regret slayed me. I was leaving again, and it seemed even harder this time. It was a painful day when I packed our things again. Doing it to them once was bad enough, but putting them through it a second time was horrendous for all of us. Ryan wrote a note to me when I was preparing to return to Wisconsin: "Please don't make us leave, Mom." I've kept that little note with me always. I cried, but there was no point in pretending. It wasn't right to stay, and this time I was leaving for good. We agreed on the same arrangements of the boys spending the school year with me and summers with Fran, so once again, I packed them up and moved them out of our home. I said goodbye to Fran and boarded a plane back to Wisconsin.

We sat on the plane in silence and tears. Ryan stared out the window, and I could see he was already missing his dad. As I watched him, my heart broke and a tear rolled down my cheek. Shaun put his little hand on my arm for comfort. It was a long flight back to Wausau. Before we landed, I reached out, touched the boys' sweet little faces, kissed them and promised everything would be okay.

When I returned to Wausau, the radio station that I had worked for offered me a sales manager's position. I remember thinking, *Me? A manager? This girl from a small town, who could barely survive when she got here?* I was proud that they trusted me with such a responsibility, and I took the job. Later on, it turned into the role of general manager, where I ran a successful AM and FM radio station—and what a great experience it was. During that time, I graduated with an associate degree in marketing. It was one of the highlights of my life.

It was around this time that I met Kevin. He was fit and muscular, had an enticing smile and beautiful blue eyes. He was introduced to me by somebody that I'd dated before. Pat set us up, and we clicked from the start. I admired Kevin's sense of adventure and spontaneity as much as I admired his good looks. On weekends, we went to Northern Wisconsin to a cottage with his two brothers, Kirk and Kraig, their girlfriends—who eventually became their wives—and other friends. We spent happy days there playing in the water and enjoying games of volleyball. During the evening we would all sit under the tall pine trees and watch the sunset. It was a place where all the cares of the world melted away. This was the life I'd wanted but had never known, and I was uplifted by the spirit of happiness and lightheartedness we shared. Was this what it was like to be young and carefree? I wanted to always be a part of this wonderful, positive energy.

Kevin and his friends loved to waterski, but I'd never tried it. I was terrified of falling into the big lake. It was clear, though, that if I was going to date Kevin, I was going to have to dredge up some courage and learn his sport. He was a good skier; he could have competed professionally. Thankfully, he was also a great teacher. In one weekend, at the age of twenty-nine, I learned to get up on two skis, drop a ski and finally, to get up on one ski and slalom.

Over the next year, we spent more time skiing the slopes on a mountain in our city, golfing, and snowmobiling than we did sleeping. The boys enjoyed all the sports with Kevin, and seeing them happy made my heart dance. He was kind, patient, and lots of fun. We couldn't get enough of each other and spent every weekend together and as many evenings during the week as we could. We explored unique restaurants and claimed some as our favorites. Kevin's family and friends brought laughter and hope into my life. I believed I could be happy again.

His family grew ginseng on the fertile farmland in Central Wisconsin. Wisconsin is home to some of the best quality ginseng in the world. Although this way of farming was different for me, I jumped in and helped during busy times. The boys enjoyed helping as well. As my connection with Kevin and his family got more intense, so did our relationship. We talked about marriage. Kevin was honest and told me he was scared of walking into a marriage with two small children. He didn't think he could do it. But, as the boys enjoyed all the adventure Kevin brought into our lives and he saw the admiration in their eyes as he patiently taught them to waterski, he fell in love with my adorable boys. His fear of fatherhood lifted, and he wanted them in his life. He loved them as if they were his own and was an amazing role model—fair, consistent, and loving.

We knew this was right and wanted to start a life together. We were committed and made our plans to get married. I had to pinch myself to believe all the wonderful changes that had come into my life. At the same time, I was afraid. It seemed that life was too good.

Kevin and I got married in Wausau in March 1990. The boys were so proud when they walked me down the aisle. It was a day of joy for all of us. We settled into life as a family in the small house we bought together. One day, Kevin brought a dog home, and the boys were beside themselves with excitement and joy—now we had a dog, a cat, and a chameleon. The kids' lives were fun and active. They were busy meeting new friends, biking, and catching frogs in the nearby pond.

A year later, they gained another brother, Jordan. The boys loved having a baby in the house, and laughter filled our home. Life was humming along, and Kevin, the children, and I were growing closer as a unit, but I knew a big change was coming. Soon, we would have to live with the agreement I made with Fran during the divorce. When Ryan was thirteen and Shaun twelve, they were to spend the school years with him and the summers with me. When we put the plan in place, Fran only lived a hundred miles away and it had seemed logical, but now I saw how disruptive it was going to be to the boys and us as a family. Sitting around that table seven years earlier making visitation plans with Fran, we had no idea he would end up living in Idaho, over 1,500 miles away.

Fran had remarried not long after he'd moved out there. He met his wife when he was helping a friend put new windows in her house. Mutual friends set up a date between them, and he married her six weeks later. She was attractive, classy, and owned a beautiful home. She appeared to have everything organized and together. Anxious to marry on her birth-day, she pulled off a complete wedding with invitations, napkins, dinner, and music in just four days. When she wanted something, she usually got her way. He was happy, but he couldn't see at the time that his new wife had a much harsher parenting style than ours. It quickly became obvious she was not fully accepting of the boys.

She had two other children and didn't treat my kids fairly. The boys were in their early teens and not allowed in the kitchen after 9:00 p.m. and were never allowed to go into her bathroom. They were growing teenagers, and at our house, when they were hungry, they could go into the kitchen and help themselves. If they needed something out of my bathroom, they could walk in and get it. They also had a lot more chores at her house, but then again maybe I was too lax in that area. I knew it was going to be a disruptive situation for them, so I tried to convince Fran that it would be too hard for the boys to adjust to living with a woman who didn't embrace them. Fran didn't see it that way, however, and I couldn't drag the boys into court to testify that they didn't want to live with their father, particularly not with his wife. I had to honor the agreement.

The boys did their best to cooperate, as they didn't want to hurt any-one, but it was so difficult for them to leave the homelife we shared with Kevin and their baby brother. We were so happy as a family and had finally settled into the rhythm of our new life. On top of that, they had to adjust to yet another school. If I'd known how hard it would be for them to live in that house, I would have fought harder, but hindsight comes at the price of foresight. Reluctantly, we packed them up for the school year and counted the days until summer when they could come back home.

This visitation arrangement was painful for Kevin, the boys, and me, and it ushered in another devastating period of my life. I felt that I had created a stable, loving home for them, and just when they'd reached the age when they needed my guidance and protection most, I had to give them up for nine months of the year. I tried to think of it as an early off-to-college experience, but we missed the big-family fun and craziness in our house something fierce. We called them often and exchanged pictures with them, but our house wasn't complete. Shaun dealt with the situation well, but Ryan rebelled. We all struggled through this time—even Fran and his wife— and it's one of my big regrets in life.

A few years passed, and Kevin and I added another precious baby boy to our family—Justin was born in June 1993. We moved to a house on a lake about thirty minutes north of Wausau. Our house was only a few feet from the water, and when we walked out of the large glass door onto a brick paver patio that followed the curve of the lawn, we were at the lake. When the older boys came home, they now had two little brothers to laugh with as well as a lake to play on.

They absolutely loved it, and enjoyed fishing off the dock. Sometimes they would just lay on their tummies in the summer sun and watch the fish swim. There was a small beach that kids spent hours playing on and building sandcastles. Jordan liked it so much he would taste the sand once in a while—I always wondered if he was lacking some mineral in his body. Even though at times we had too many frogs and turtles, after a few days, they'd set them free. The boys were soon waterskiing well, which gave us something special to share. I loved it when they were all home at the same time—the four boys made for a rowdy, happy household, just the way I'd always imagined family life could be.

Ryan continued to have difficulty living with his dad and stepmom, so in time he moved back to Wisconsin. It was a hard decision for him to leave Shaun behind, but he couldn't do it anymore. There was just too much friction in the house. Although he loved his little brothers, being separated from Shaun was harder than he had imagined. He missed his best friend, and I could see he was angry about the situation.

It was about this time I reached a turning point in my career trajectory. One year, right before Christmas, I was asked to lay off a couple of people who worked at the radio station. I'd never had a problem talking with the staff about performance reviews and layoffs that were necessary; however, this one was different. It was Christmas. At that point, I asked myself what I wanted to do? I did some soul searching and decided I wanted more control over what happened in my workplace. Owning my own business was the answer. After doing some research, I approached a woman in town who ran an advertising agency with one part-time copywriter. Chris's personality and skill set were different from mine, and she felt I would be useful to strengthen her company.

Over the next six months, we met regularly and put a deal together to buy out her partner. He was satisfied with the arrangement, and Chris and I became equal partners. Chris oversaw the creative side, including design and copy, and I oversaw the business aspect, focusing on sales and billing.

We had a team approach to strategy and campaign concepts. It worked out just right for us and for our small team, which grew and flourished.

The time came when Kevin and I decided to build a home back in Wausau. We missed the town and our friends who lived there, and we were constantly driving back to see them. The two youngest boys were approaching school age, and we wanted to shorten our commute to their schools and our jobs. Kevin and I had a thirty-minute drive to work, and our schedules were demanding. He was a union sheet metal welder and worked in the ginseng fields every night and on the weekends. My business was growing, and my job called for extra-long days, so we sold our home and moved into a rental, while we built our dream house on Wausau's west side. The setting we chose was breathtaking, situated on top of a hill and nestled among tall oak and maple trees. It had three-stories and four-bedrooms and was in a lovely neighborhood on five acres. It was two miles from work, and we couldn't have been more excited. Kevin and I planned every detail from the foundation to the roof and everything in between. The décor we chose was beautiful, accented by an abundance of natural light. It was like walking into an art gallery.

Other aspects of our lives improved as well, and the boys thrived. Shortly after Shaun graduated from high school in Idaho, he moved back to Wisconsin with us. It was so nice to have him home again. All the boys enjoyed being reunited. Fran ended his difficult second marriage and found love with a partner that he was more compatible with. They married, moved back to Northern Wisconsin, and built a home together. Fran's path may have taken him out West for a while, but he had found his way back to Wisconsin. It was so much better for everybody.

Things became more friendly between Fran and me, but it took years before we could have a proper conversation. A turning point came when I told him I forgave him for verbally mistreating me so harshly, and asked for his forgiveness of my mistakes as well. I explained that I was so young and had needed to get away from all the hurt, pain, and sadness. We both took responsibility for our part in the disintegration of our relationship. After that conversation, things began shifting, and Fran was more cordial with me and became good friends with Kevin. It meant so much to Shaun in particular that his two fathers were friendly with each other.

Kevin, Fran, Shaun, and some friends began going on fishing trips to Canada together. It took time, but Ryan began to heal from the wounds inflicted by Fran's prior marriage, and Ryan and his dad became close again.

In fact, Ryan followed in Fran's footsteps and excelled as a carpenter. Today, they have a close relationship and work together in construction.

Coming to a point of forgiveness worked miracles in our lives. Fran and I now respect and understand each other and are truly good friends. We both understand now that our marriage could have been strong if we'd had the maturity and counseling we needed to cope with the stress we were under. And yet, our paths were destined to go in different directions. We have learned and changed in so many ways, and I'm so happy that we found the right people to love. Because of the way things unfolded, I was blessed with a good husband and two more wonderful sons—I wouldn't change that for the world. When we spend time with each other and our families are all together, it feels like time is standing still. We are at peace, and for that, I am eternally grateful.

CHAPTER FIVE

SHAUN GROWS UP

I couldn't love you any more than I do.
—Cindy Baumann

AS SHAUN GREW, his sensitive nature matured with him. He cared for and nurtured people around him. He loved plants and animals and was eager to play outdoors, to enjoy the moment, and to just live. I guess I handed down to him the trait of bringing home animals. Shaun brought his first dog home, and we all fell in love with the sweetness of Ice. One look into those deep blue eyes, and we agreed to keep her. She was a husky and Australian shepherd mix, and in no time she had woven herself into our hearts. Shortly after, Shaun brought home another dog, a black lab he named Kennan. On the weekends when we headed up north, she would spend hours wading in the shallow water trying to catch fish.

Even though Shaun suffered physical and emotional scars that lived with him far beyond his childhood illness, there was never a "Why me?" attitude. When he was an adolescent, however, the physical scars started to bother him. The radiation had stunted the bone growth in his chest, leaving the right side two-thirds smaller than the left. He was monitored to make sure it didn't apply pressure or pull on his spine as he matured. He was very health-conscious about what he ate, and he worked out like crazy to build muscle around the deformity in his chest.

During his late teens, doctors discussed sending him to a specialist for a treatment called muscle weaving, but there were no guarantees that it would help. In the end, we decided as a family not to put him through another procedure. Instead, he chose to work hard to camouflage it through exercise. The transformation of his body amazed the doctors and everybody around him. True to his nature, he had made the best of every situation life put in front of him. He was determined, and God helped him get there. By the time he was twenty-one, if he had a shirt on, you couldn't tell that his chest was uneven.

Shaun was kind, compassionate, respectful, and selfless with his time. If somebody needed him, he was there. The kid never once disrespected me, even during his teenage years. And he remembered my birthday and Mother's Day with a card every year. His only bad habit was a sweet tooth. If I didn't bake, he'd be in the kitchen mixing up cookies or bars himself. His favorite was no-bake chocolate oatmeal cookies. His brothers loved it when he satisfied his craving because they were never far behind, and there was always plenty to go around. He loved sports and was a natural in everything he tried. In school, he played hockey and was darn good at it. I still have his stick and will always treasure it. Maybe someday, one of the grandchildren will play and want to have it to bring them luck.

Shaun and I got along well because we were so alike. Neither of us could sit still, and we loved to tease each other. In the morning, we would be in the kitchen, he would be mixing up a healthy breakfast that always included eggs, and I would be pouring my first cup of strong coffee.

He'd say, "Mom, when you get home from work, what are you baking me? How about a batch of peanut butter chocolate chip cookies, or some chocolate no-bake cookies?"

I would just smile and say, "Or if you have time, you can whip something up for me? I would be fine with either of those choices."

He enjoyed a cold glass of milk with his warm cookies, and I'd get a text message marked "Urgent," reminding me to pick milk up on my way home.

Both Shaun and I were determined to succeed at whatever we did. It didn't matter how much work it took to get there; we didn't give up until we reached our goal. Still, we were different enough to complement each other. He was such a good listener and helped me learn important things in life, such as being more patient and selfless and to think before I speak. The idea of being "in the present moment" was nothing new to Shaun—

that was his only way. He had wisdom beyond his years, and when he loved somebody, he loved them with all his heart. Along with Ryan, Shaun liked to introduce Jordan and Justin to new adventures. The younger boys loved the attention of their big brothers, and the bonds were strong. It wasn't always easy being the mother of four active boys, but there was never a dull moment in our house!

There was so much joy in my life brought in by this little boy who grew to be a friend as well. With our common interests, our lives intertwined naturally, and we shared fun times and laughter over the years. There was one incident regarding Shaun's hair that neither of us forgot and often laughed about. As an adult, Shaun was particular about his hair, and kept it clean and styled every day. One Saturday, he was due a haircut and didn't want to wait until Monday, so he asked me if I could try. I jokingly told him this was not my specialty, and I didn't remember that clause in my "Being a Mother" contract, but he just laughed and said he would talk me through it. I grabbed the clippers, and I was doing okay until I started on the back of his head. My hand slipped, and I cut a section too short.

I tried pulling on the hair around it to cover the spot, but he caught on. "Mom, what happened?"

Knowing how fussy he was with his hair, I said, "It's fine. Besides it's at the back, so you won't even see it."

We laughed so hard that day as I struggled to complete his haircut. He'd trusted me with those clippers, and it was another way of spending time together. We enjoyed each other's company. I was always sure of Shaun's love for me, and he was sure of mine.

He took care of his appearance and had a way with his clothes. Being the good-looking kid he was, he had a couple of girlfriends and even experienced a big heartbreak. After that, he gave up on girls for a while and concentrated on going to college, holding down a part-time job, spending time with his brothers, and working out at the gym.

We worried about him until Julia came into his life. I remember the night they met. Some friends from school invited him to a party, and he agreed to go out and have fun. The party was better than he anticipated when he laid eyes on Julia. She was a beautiful, dark-haired girl with deep brown eyes and golden, bronzed skin. Shaun told us later that the moment they were introduced, she owned his heart, and he knew she was the one. God had brought her into his life. After watching Shaun being single for so long, I knew he was afraid to give his heart away for fear he could get hurt again, but clearly things had changed. The light in his eyes told me everything. This was true love.

Julia attended college forty minutes away, where she was studying to become a teacher. She was home every weekend to spend time with her parents who, conveniently, lived two miles away from us. When Shaun met her parents, he was very nervous. Her father was a professor at the same university Shaun attended. He seemed quiet and reserved, but they found common ground and Shaun learned he was quite friendly and had a wonderful sense of humor. After the first dinner with them, he was even more sure about his future with Julia. Our families connected, and Julia spent weekends up north with us at the cabin. She added so much sparkle to our lives. We all fell in love with her.

After two years, Shaun transferred to the University of Wisconsin–Madison in preparation for entering medical school, and Julia wanted to join him. She accepted a bilingual teaching position in Madison so they could be together. They got engaged, and after dating four years, our families gathered on Rib Mountain in Wausau, Wisconsin on a glorious summer day to watch them become husband and wife. The setting was breathtaking; you can see forever up there. We truly felt like we were in the heavens.

Julia was stunning in her beautiful white dress against her golden skin, and Shaun looked so handsome in his bright white shirt and black tuxedo. The bridesmaids wore a soft pastel pink, and Julia carried magenta pink roses that had been flown in from Ecuador, where her mom was from. Many of her Ecuadoran family members flew in to attend. Out of respect for them, the ceremony was conducted in both English and Spanish. When Shaun stood at the front and watched his beautiful bride walk down the aisle, he cried, and from that moment on, there wasn't a dry eye at the ceremony. One of the songs at the wedding was Jack Johnson's "Better Together" . . . and that's exactly how it was for those two. There was so much love between them, you could feel it the second you saw them.

Life was perfect and couldn't get any better. We knew Shaun and Julia would love each other forever, but nobody could have guessed how short their time together would be.

CHAPTER SIX

THE ULTIMATE LOSS

The trouble is... you think you have time.
—Jack Kornfield

IT WAS THE night before Thanksgiving in 2007, and family members were arriving home for the celebration. Thanksgiving was traditionally a big holiday for us. We gathered at my parents' house, and like always we were so happy for the chance to be together. Shaun and his wife, Julia, were coming home from Madison and, as usual, I was looking forward to seeing them. They had only been married three months, and yet they came home to Wausau nearly every weekend. Julia spent time with her family, and Shaun would do the same and then we'd often get together. We were grateful the newlyweds wanted to share so much of their time with us.

On Thanksgiving Day, Shaun and Julia came to my parents' house. We were sitting around the table, enjoying each other's company when Shaun told everybody he'd landed a part-time job at Dick's Sporting Goods. He had been studying for his MCAT (Medical College Admission Test) and was looking for a job to help with the expenses. With approximately 45,000 students in Madison, there was a lot of competition among the student population, so this was big news. He also announced that he'd secured a volunteer position in the emergency room at Meriter Hospital. Knowing this was a great experience for him on his way to becoming a doctor, I was delighted. Happiness and excitement shone in his eyes. Everything was falling into place.

I remember how Julia laughed as she told us the nickname the staff at his job had given Shaun. He had been there a couple of weeks and they were already calling him "Hollywood" because he was so careful with his appearance. He wore a long-sleeved buttoned-up shirt with *two* t-shirts underneath. He was still self-conscious about his chest and felt by double layering, it camouflaged any imperfections left by the radiation treatments. His hair was always spiked on top—it looked perfect every time we saw him. I wondered if he had a lingering memory of losing his hair during cancer, which made him appreciate every strand more than other people in his peer group. He didn't think of himself as a pretty boy—but he was.

That day was like every other Thanksgiving Day. We each brought a dish to share and had a delicious dinner. We played board games and had our normal two tables of cards going on simultaneously. Shortly after we finished eating, Shaun and Julia left to spend the evening with her family, but returned to our house to sleep, slipping in late after we were all in bed. On Black Friday, the day after Thanksgiving, I went shopping with my sisters, as we'd always done. Shaun had an appointment to get new tires on Julia's car—it was the day of the mega deals, so everybody was busy with something.

At 11:30, Shaun called and asked me what I was doing. I was trying on boots in a large department store. It was an ordinary mother and son conversation, and I'll never forget where I was at that time, or the words we exchanged.

"Are you shopping with your sisters, Mom?"

"Yes, what are you doing?"

"Having lunch with Julia's family."

And that was it—just a brief normal conversation. If I had known it was the last time I would ever speak to my son, what would I have said? "What are you doing this evening? Would you and Julia like to join us for dinner like you did last year? We would love to have both of you," or "I love you so much, Shaun. You are a good son and I'm blessed to have you in my life."

But those words weren't spoken. Instead, when I arrived home, Jordan said, "You just missed Shaun. He decided at the last minute to go hunting with his dad, Ryan, and Maria."

I was surprised that Shaun had gone with them. He had told me he was staying home to work on his trailer, but then he always loved doing things with his brother, dad, and relatives. I had a missed call from him on my cell phone, so I tried to reach him but got his voicemail.

The next morning, I treated my sisters to strong coffee and introduced them to Shaun's favorite breakfast—waffles smothered in peanut butter and drizzled with maple syrup. After breakfast, it was time for everybody to get back to reality. My sisters went back to Mom and Dad's house to rescue them from their kids, knowing they'd be ready for a break. It was great getting all the cousins together, but like all kids, they were active. I jumped in the shower and got dressed before heading over to my mom's house to pick up Justin.

Just when I was ready to leave the house, the phone rang. It was Ryan's wife, Maria, and she was crying so hard that I could barely make out what she was saying. She said, "There's been a terrible accident—it's Shaun."

Everything in me froze. Time stood still. I didn't ask her what had happened or how serious it was. I knew he was hunting with a group, and deep inside I feared he'd been shot. I was too afraid to hear the details. All I wanted to know was where they were taking him. The only thing that mattered was finding him and holding him in my arms. However bad it might be, I believed that my love could heal him, just as it had done when he was a baby.

She said an ambulance was taking him to Ladysmith, and then they'd airlift him to Marshfield. I told her to call Julia and let her know that I would pick her up, then asked Jordan to drive us to Marshfield to meet them there. It was a lot to ask of a young man—he was only sixteen and had just gotten his driver's license. His older brother was injured, and his mother and sister-in-law were beside themselves, but he was brave and did what he had to. Today, I understand how hard that was for him.

The hospital was an hour away, and we hoped Shaun would be there when we arrived. It was a great hospital, and we believed he would be all right. It was getting him there that scared me—I knew the area in Kennan, Wisconsin, where he was shot. It was desolate and about an hour away from the nearest hospital, which was not equipped to deal with something of this magnitude. I wished it were possible to airlift him straight to Marshfield, but it wasn't. They needed to get him to the closest hospital and then transport him. Our drive there was tough, but we didn't let ourselves think that he wouldn't make it.

While Jordan drove, I was curled up in a ball on the front seat. Julia was wrapped in her mother's arms in the back, and her father and brother followed in a separate car. It was a cloudy winter day, and a sudden beam of bright white light appeared on the horizon. I looked up at it in the sky, and a terrible dread swept over me. I had the distinct feeling that I was watching the departure of my son's soul. I could feel him leaving us, and I was terrified. It was as if I knew the truth but couldn't let myself consider it. I've never forgotten that vision.

When we arrived at the hospital, I couldn't wait to see Shaun and hold him tight. We rushed into the emergency room, but they said he hadn't arrived yet and they didn't have any information for us. I begged them to call the first hospital where the helicopter was bringing him from to see when he would be arriving. They spoke to somebody at the other hospital and said they had some new information for us. We were taken into a very small room, and it was then that our nightmare turned.

The chaplain looked at us and said, "He won't be transported here. He didn't make it."

I couldn't comprehend her words. How could the chaplain just blurt this out? I'll never forget that little room and who was in there with me: Julia and her parents, Elba and Ron, her brother David, Jordan, and myself.

Julia and I screamed and fell to the floor, and everybody burst into tears. How could Shaun be gone? What had happened to our lives? They told us to go home because we wouldn't be able to see him and there was nothing that we could do. We were left without purpose. We pulled ourselves off the floor, got back in our cars, and somehow managed the hour-long trip back home. None of us talked; we were in shock. We couldn't believe this had happened to our Shaun and had no idea what we were about to go through.

We were almost home when my sister called and told us to go to the hospital where Shaun's body was being held. They wanted Julia and I to see him before they took him to a larger hospital for the autopsy. We re-routed, and poor Jordan had to drive again, as none of us could function. I believe Shaun gave his younger brother the strength he needed to handle the driving that day. The two-hour trip was pure misery, but I couldn't help but notice the beauty of the sky filled with bright orange and fiery red streaks of light. I'd never seen a sunset like it—the colors were so vibrant and vivid. I wondered how I could notice such a trivial thing through my tears, but something was pulling my attention upward. I think it was Shaun asking me to look up at the glory of God's handiwork.

We arrived at the hospital, and when I looked at the entrance, I understood why we were told to come. I was hysterical and screaming, "I know why you brought me here—you want me to accept this, and I won't." I grabbed the frame of the door and braced myself, refusing to walk in. They had to pull me through the doors into the hospital. The whole family was there; they lined the white stark walls leading to his room. Julia went in first and I can still hear her cries. They were together for four years and had been married for just three short months. My heart broke for her; their entire future full of wonderful dreams and plans was gone.

After Julia, it was my turn. I walked in and there he was—my precious son, lying peacefully. I waited for his stunning blue eyes to open and meet mine. Surely they would—they had to. He looked as though he was sleeping, like he would wake up at any moment. His beautiful blond hair was styled. His eyelashes were so long, you could comb them. I leaned over and kissed his face. The boy I had given birth to, had nursed for fifteen months, had loved so deeply, and protected through years of cancer treatments, was gone.

I'd held him in my arms so many times that my body knew the shape of him. He was so cold. The chill spread through the room. It was the kind of cold that you can't warm up. I could almost see my breath hovering over his body—or was that his spirit? Everything was so surreal. Time was suspended in silence. I could see myself touching his hand as if I was looking at us from afar.

I traced his beautiful fingers. They were long and slender; I'd always thought he had the hands of a surgeon. I studied his face, his hands, and his feet, thinking about how I wouldn't be able to see them again. I focused on his chest, hoping to see it rise. I waited for him to take a breath and speak again, to hear him say, "Mom." I pressed my cheek against his face, and I knew for certain that the life in my boy was gone. Somebody had taken him away from me in one split second on that cold Wisconsin day. Didn't they see him in the woods? Why would they shoot at a random sound? How could they not know that sound was my son, my wonderful son, and that he was loved by so many people?

I will never forget the clothes I had on as I wept over his body. I'll never wear them again, but I'll keep them forever because they were the last articles of my clothing to touch my son. They asked us if we wanted to donate some of his organs. My heart slumped; I couldn't believe we were having this conversation. With his giving spirit, we knew Shaun would want to help somebody else, so we agreed.

The shock of everything overwhelmed me, and I started shaking all over, my teeth chattering uncontrollably. A nurse came with a wheelchair and took me out of his room before they took his body for organ donation.

The ride home was a blur. I cried all the way back and throughout the night, unable to fathom what had happened. The crying was endless and intense—I couldn't catch my breath. I could taste the vomit in my throat and could feel the pain in my heart. The next day, my doctor visited and sat with me on the edge of my bed. She was more than my doctor; she was my friend. She knew how much I loved and worried about my kids. We even went through a pregnancy together. I trusted her, and on that day, I needed her to be there. It meant so much that she was by my side.

Home would never feel the way it once had. It wasn't complete. There would always be a missing piece. The sound of his footsteps walking above my bedroom ceiling, the water he splashed in the sink styling his hair, the chair he sat on in the kitchen. He was all over our house, and I had to go home to emptiness.

Julia and Shaun had slept there the night before—how could I ever wash their bedding? I couldn't imagine what she was feeling, knowing that was the last time she would ever sleep with her husband. They'd had the kind of relationship that you always wished for your children. The respect and love between them was a gift. I told Julia that she was like an angel to him after everything he'd endured, and she responded, "He's *my* angel." She was so lovely, and we called her "Sweet Julia." Her heart was kind, and her soul was good. I felt blessed to have her in our family. Shaun loved her so much and that in itself made me happy. Everybody felt the same way about her—Jordan and Justin admired her so much. I was full of grief for her as well as myself.

From various accounts and points of view, I pieced together the story of what happened to cause Shaun's death. He'd joined his brother and dad on a deer drive, where hunters push the deer through the woods toward people who are standing on post. The leader in charge of the drive puts hunters called posters throughout the woods. The leader is supposed to explain to each poster where the others are so that they know where they should shoot. The posters are on stand while the other hunters drive the deer toward them.

A deer drive is an unpredictable and chaotic experience. In the drama of the moment, my son was shot by a hunter who was placed next to him. This man was a friend of the leader but a stranger to us. On the last drive of the day, on November 24, 2007, this man was probably shooting at a deer and accidentally hit my son. Because of that, we lost a son, husband, brother, grandson, nephew, cousin, and friend.

I would learn later that Fran, for reasons he couldn't understand, had been uncomfortable about going hunting that day, All morning he had an unsafe feeling, a premonition shared by our daughter-in-law, Maria. He sensed that God was giving him subtle signs, but he didn't know what to make of them. At one point, Fran told Ryan and Maria, "After this deer drive, we are done."

Facing life without Shaun was unthinkable for everybody who knew him. He was the glue in our family—the one all the brothers would go to for help or just to talk. Since Ryan and Shaun were only fifteen months apart, they were best friends. They went through a lot together as young- sters—Shaun's illness, the divorce, the custody living situation, and our blended family. As they grew older, they'd depended on each other more. They were each other's strength when times were tough. They could get through anything, as long as they had each other.

Shaun had a special bond with his younger brothers too. He'd taught Justin how to bow hunt and had promised to help him build an enter- tainment center, and he'd helped Jordan with more complex projects, such as working on an engine. Shaun's room was next door to Jordan's, and every night between 9:30 and 10:00, I would hear them talking. After Shaun moved to Madison, they would continue their conversations over the phone almost every night. I don't know what they talked about, but it meant so much to know how strong that brotherly love was. After the ac- cident, Jordan's room was quiet at night. It was a silence that tore my heart to pieces.

I worried so much about what the boys were going through. They all grieved deeply, wishing they'd had more time with Shaun. Jordan was moody and difficult to talk to. Later, he apologized and said he was angry and didn't know what to do with his feelings. On the other hand, Ryan became quiet and withdrawn. He was with Shaun the day of the accident and fought to save his life. He, along with his cousin who was a nurse, gave Shaun mouth-to-mouth resuscitation to keep him alive until the para- medics arrived. With tears running down his face, Ryan breathed every ounce of life he could into Shaun. I can't imagine the helplessness he felt watching the brother he loved slowly fade away. It's an experience that will haunt Ryan forever.

My husband, Kevin, also struggled terribly with the loss of the boy he'd helped raise. He had always admired Shaun's energy and drive in life. It was like Shaun was making up for lost time and was always on the go and urging others to do the same. You'd never find him just sitting around watching TV—he'd get everyone on their feet and out the door. Kevin and Shaun had shared so many common interests. They'd spent most of their time together, building things out of stainless steel and wood, traveling out West on hunting trips, boating, skiing, and never missing their annual fishing trip to Canada. Most importantly, they'd shared a love for skiing on the lake. It was Shaun's goal to waterski as well as Kevin, and he was getting mighty close before he died. He would have reached his goal if he'd had more time to practice.

It made me so happy to see how much Kevin and Shaun loved talking to each other. Shaun would go out of his way to get some phone time with Kevin. Because Kevin punched a clock, he couldn't talk freely on the phone throughout the day, so he and Shaun would make plans several times a week to call each other during his lunch hour or his morning break.

Shaun had enriched everybody's life. A split-second mistake in the woods had changed that forever. Our dreams were shattered; everything we had known and hoped for was taken away in an instant. The loss of Shaun would come to define us all.

Journal Entry
December 8, 2007
Dear Shaun,

I miss you so much! I sure hope you know how very much I love you. Did you know how proud I was of you? Did I tell you how handsome you were? Did I thank you enough? I wish I could have you back, I want to hold you so tight and feel your warm face next to mine. I'm sorry I missed you Friday night. Maybe, I could have talked you into staying home. I didn't get our weekend, we always managed to find some time together. I treasured each moment with you. I'm so heartbroken, I can't imagine life without you. I always thought you would be with us forever.

How do we live without you? Can you help us from heaven? I'm so lonely and sad, and I just wish you would visit me and tell me you are happy and with me all the time. I'm sorry for being busy the last couple of weeks, I would give anything to have that time back. Julia is broken, she loved you so much, it hurts me to see her like this. It's like she is a part of me. I promise to love and take care of her for you. Please send her a sign so she can find peace.

This has been a horrible nightmare and your entire family is deeply hurt. Shaun . . . if I know you are happy, I can someday find a way to live without you. All I ever wanted was to love you and for you to be happy. Please tell me you are happy. I don't think I could love you any more than I do. When I'm off guard, I catch myself rocking you like I did when you were a baby. It breaks my heart to not have you with me. How can life change so fast? Help me live a good life so I can be in heaven with you someday. Guide me, give me direction and purpose. Please come to me. I miss you so much. I'll write to you again soon. With all my Love . . .

Mom xxx

CHAPTER SEVEN

IN A MILLION LITTLE PIECES

No one ever told me that grief felt like fear.
—C. S. Lewis

LIFE IS INHERENTLY challenging. Most people have known their share of loss and heartache, and I was no different. The fire, Shaun's childhood cancer, and my divorce had taken their toll, but I had somehow managed to emerge intact and eager to participate in everything life had to offer. Throughout it all I was resilient and evolved stronger on the other side. However, when Shaun was killed, I couldn't function. Everything came to a standstill. I couldn't take it anymore. Everything I had relied on before—faith, family, work, friends, and my natural optimistic spirit—couldn't penetrate the agony I felt. None of my "life tools" worked, and the bearings that held my life together collapsed. I fell hard, and I couldn't get back up. For me, losing my child was the ultimate loss. I felt as though I'd shattered into a million pieces.

I didn't leave my room and rarely got out of bed except to handle the funeral arrangements and attend the services. I'll never forget the day I picked up Julia at her house and we went to the funeral home together. When her eyes met mine, the unspeakable sadness we shared was all we could see. How I wanted to bring Shaun back to her so I could see her beautiful, warm smile once again. We went through the motions of planning his funeral automatically without internalizing what had happened. I believe the only way anybody gets through something like this is by being in a state of shock. You must be—how else can you decide how you are going to bury your child?

When the funeral director asked us the usual question—burial or cremation—Julia and I looked at each other with a blank stare. Shaun had never talked about what he wanted us to do if he died. Why would he be thinking about such things? He was only twenty-six. I asked Julia what she thought he'd want, and she said cremation, so we went with that; either option was equally unimaginable to us. It didn't matter to me, and I was grateful that his wife had the strength to decide for us. They suggested an open casket before the cremation. I guess it was recommended due to his age, or maybe they were trying to get us to accept his death. We picked out a casket, and Kevin decided to make a stainless-steel urn for him along with a few small personal urns for us to keep some of his ashes in. On the front of the urn, it read:

Our Gift from God
Shaun L. Winter
Sept 8, 1981 – Nov 24, 2007
WE WILL LOVE YOU FOREVER

I gave the funeral director my confirmation cross, which had made it through the fire, to include in his cremation. It felt as though I was including a piece of protection to go with him. I asked them to put it in the small personal urn so I could keep them together, knowing they had both survived so much. I keep the little urn in my bedroom on my dresser so he can be close to me and watch over me while I sleep. I don't know what else to do with him. It's sad when all you have left of somebody you adore is ashes.

I brought a picture of Shaun and asked the director to make sure he looked good and to style his hair. We picked out a pair of jeans, a blue-striped long-sleeve shirt, and a white undershirt. He also had a pair of leather shoes he liked a lot. It was all done mechanically and methodically, as if we were in a daze.

The next thing we had to consider was food. What would we serve after the funeral? Did we want chicken, ham, or beef? Mashed potatoes? Dessert? All I could think was, Are you kidding me? I couldn't care less if people ate; nothing like that mattered. I came out of my state of constant numbness with brief flashes of anger, wondering how people would be able to enjoy a lunch when I'd left my son in a casket.

There was a visitor at the wake who I believe was an angel. He came through the line and told me he had been a teacher of Shaun's when he was in elementary school. He said that recently he'd been looking at some of my son's artwork and would send it on to me. I assumed he was retiring and had been reviewing the files he had saved. Shaun always worked hard at his art, striving to compete with Ryan, who had a real artistic flair. He always said he wanted to "make the wall" in my office where I hung some of their best work. He made a special effort with Mother's Day cards and gifts—they always expressed so much love and appreciation. When he got older, he made several bird houses. One of them looks like a mini log cabin. I can't bring myself to set it outside, so it will never be used as a bird house—the sparrows' loss, but one that I feel is forgivable. When we sold our house, the buyers were so impressed with it that they wanted to buy it, but it wasn't for sale. I will treasure it forever.

Before Shaun's teacher left, he hugged me. As I looked into his eyes, I saw something special shining there. I watched for the promised artwork for months but never received it. It definitely would have made the wall if I had. I wasn't surprised it didn't arrive. I'd had a feeling this was not a former teacher, but an angel letting me know Shaun was checking in on me from Heaven. Shaun had only been in his class for a year, and that was sixteen years ago. When this man looked into my eyes, it was like Shaun was with him. I like to think that in Heaven my son can create all the beautiful art he can imagine.

On the day of the funeral, I could barely function enough to dress myself. My friends told me we would have a large crowd of people and should be prepared, so we made the necessary decisions. My friends were right—people came from near and far to honor my son. His spirit of love and kindness had touched so many hearts, and they wanted to express their support for us and their respect for him.

Before I experienced a loss of this magnitude firsthand, I didn't think people noticed who came to a funeral. Now I know they do. I can remember everybody who attended. Some of our friends traveled across the country to be there. Doctors and a very special nurse who cared for Shaun when he had cancer as a baby came to show their respects. After twenty-six years, they hadn't forgotten us. We were the family who had fought so hard to save our little boy, only to lose him just as he'd fully entered adulthood.

Family, friends, new clients and old clients, and people we hadn't seen in years, as well as our closest friends—they were all there. It was one of the largest funerals St. Anne's Church had ever seen. There is power in a group that large. It was a tangible force, and I felt like they were all holding me up. Their presence meant the world to us.

The funeral home and the church overflowed with flowers. The love we felt behind each bouquet and lovingly signed card deeply touched our hearts. I didn't want the casket in the normal position at the front of the church. It had to be in a special place. I wanted it in front of the stained-glass windows near the beautiful baptismal area where the water falls from the font into a large immersion pool. He was my baby, and I thought this was the best place for him. The sun was shining through the colorful stained glass as it graced Shaun's face. Julia approached the coffin and bent down over Shaun's body for her final goodbye. When she did, her nose bled and trickled blood on his shirt across the collar. It was as if a part of her poured onto his body to go with him. The sight of the blood on his shirt was difficult to see, but strangely, it was beautiful. I rested my face on his chest and realized that the body lying in the casket no longer felt like my son. I knew his soul had traveled on. Still, it was my way of touching him with my love one last time.

Julia's father, Ron, wrote and read the eulogy. It was so insightful and expressed so much about Shaun's true nature. I think my favorite line was: "Julia liked to say that a woman can know how a man will treat his wife by the way he treats his mother, and Julia saw an extremely strong bond of love and respect between Shaun and Cindy. We have always tried to instill in our children the importance of strong family ties, and we were happy to see that Shaun was raised the same way."

Ron recommended that we live our lives by following Shaun's example, then read a list of beautiful attributes that reflected the way Shaun lived his life:

- Be fit, work out, eat healthy, take care of your body.
- Be generous with your time. Be helpful in any way you can.
- Be curious and intellectually active. Work to figure things out and always ask questions.
- Enjoy life, have fun.
- Be outdoors as much as possible, enjoy and cherish nature.
- Love animals and plants, for they add much to our lives.

- Be creative and productive—make things for yourself and others.
- Be honest, tell people what you think, never hurt them, and always encourage them.
- Honor your parents and your spouse.
- Always have time for your friends and family. Cherish them and keep them close.
- Don't waste time numbing your mind or worrying about trivial things.
- Life is precious.

Before the service, they moved the casket to the front of the church and blessed it. All the children brought a flower to his casket. Shaun was the second oldest grandchild, and they all admired him. It was unbearably sad to see all those children and young adults carrying yellow roses, one of Shaun's favorite kind, up the aisle. A friend sang the "Prayer of Saint Francis" in his memory. Like St. Francis, Shaun loved animals and nature. The lyrics are so beautiful, and they encourage us to be instruments of happiness and peace.

When the service was over, they put a cloth over the casket before the pallbearers stepped forward to carry his body out. I can't describe what I felt when I saw Shaun's best man from his wedding three months before, lean down to pick up that casket. His brothers and brother-in-law joined him, and they all wept as they walked out carrying the boy they loved so much. Julia and I walked out behind them, holding one another up. Out of the corner of my eye, I saw a dear friend of mine, Brian, who was the executive director of the Boys and Girls Club. I was on the board of the organization for years, and he knows how much I love my children. He knew this loss could kill me. His face was the picture of compassion, and I felt him hug me from a distance. I felt such love from everybody in the church, but they couldn't bring my son back. No matter how much they loved us, nobody could.

Journal Entry
January 5, 2008
Dear Shaun,

Please tell me you will be waiting for me. Some days I feel I'm just waiting to die. I have had so much pain in my heart. I don't know how to live again. I miss your life so much. I feel very far away from you. How can God keep us so far apart? Can't he see how much I'm hurting? I always felt bad when I heard someone lost a child, but I could never have imagined the hell they would be forced to live through. Will there ever be a day when I don't think of you every waking moment? I feel bad for the boys, too. They miss you. You were such a big part of everyone's life. That is what made you so special. I miss you.

Love you,
Mom

THE PRAYER OF SAINT FRANCIS

Lord, make me an instrument of your peace
Where there is hatred, let me sow love
Where there is injury, pardon
Where there is doubt, faith
Where there is despair, hope
Where there is darkness, light
And where there is sadness, joy
O Divine Master, grant that I may
Not so much seek to be consoled as to console;
To be understood, as to understand
To be loved, as to love
For it is in giving that we receive
And it's in pardoning that we are pardoned
And it's in dying that we are born to Eternal Life.
Amen.

CHAPTER EIGHT

AFTER THE FUNERAL

I wish that I could love you back to life.
—A. A. Giannone

AFTER THE FUNERAL, our mailbox stayed full of messages for weeks. Some of them were from people we'd never met but they had known and admired Shaun. Others were from friends who were close to the family. Dinner showed up at the door, people came by offering to do anything we needed, and angel statues were even dropped off in our front yard. We received keepsakes such as a memory box with a framed picture of Shaun and a beautiful verse, albums full of pictures, and all kinds of cards, crosses, and letters that I will keep for the rest of my life. We also received many cards with handwritten notes.

I don't know how we would have made it through the aftermath of Shaun's death without the continuous support of our thoughtful friends and neighbors. I realize not everyone has this kind of support around them in times of need, and I'll forever be humbled and grateful for all that was done for us. The following message from our dear friends Roger and Susan rang so true: "When someone leaves this earth, the greater the pain we feel, means the greater the love we feel for them."

Sometimes people came by and just sat with us in silence, not asking us to take part in the conversation or entertain them in any way. Their presence helped to ease the emptiness; it felt so much better when the house was full. Our place had always been busy, full of activity and constant family traffic. Now, I was afraid to be alone. Just knowing somebody else was in the house meant more than they could know. It helped keep the suffocating panic that descended upon me at bay.

I learned a great deal from being at the receiving end of the kindness of others. I realized how the smallest gesture or briefest visit can convey a tremendous amount of strength and love when a person is grieving. Because of the state of shock I was in, I wasn't able to respond properly to all those who cared for us at that time. I hope they know that their generosity and compassion will forever be remembered with profound appreciation.

It seemed like the funeral had barely ended when it was time to pick up Shaun's ashes. Julia and I went together, and thank God we had each other. When we walked out of the funeral home carrying the stainless-steel urn, all we could do was look at each other and weep. How could this be all we had left of somebody we had loved so tremendously? How could we go on without hearing his voice, hugging him, and looking into his beautiful blue eyes? I believed in heaven and knew he was there, existing in a spiritual form, but the idea of living without his physical presence was unthinkable. Plain and simple, our bodies missed his body, and we knew it would always be so.

It took me a long time to quit thinking about the act of cremation. I knew it wasn't logical, but I prayed he didn't feel anything. Maybe we should have buried him instead—but would that have been any easier? I couldn't have left the graveside if I knew he was in a coffin. I'd have wanted to rescue him from the cold ground. I was tormented by thoughts I knew were irrational. It was hard to believe, but I was angry at him. Shaun was supposed to be with me as I grew old, and he was gone. How could he leave me without even saying goodbye? He had always been part of all our future dreams.

When we bought land on a lake up north, he said, "Mom, save that lot alongside you for me to build a house. I want to live next to you."

Shaun loved everything about the summer season—family, friends, music, sunshine, and laughter. I knew he would be at the lake with us every summer. He just wanted to have fun, and he made sure everybody else did too. I'll never forget the time we spent there together a few weeks before he died. It can be quite cold in September on a lake in Wisconsin, and I was trying my best to get out of doing my ski run, but Shaun wasn't having it. He turned to me and said, "Come on, Mom, get out of the boat.

You aren't an old lady yet. You'll feel better when you're done."

How could I resist his smile? I jumped into the water and screamed when the shock of the cold penetrated my wet suit.

He laughed and said, "It will get better, Mom. You'll adjust."

I pulled myself out of the freezing water, got up on my ski, and cut against the wake, feeling invigorated and pleased with myself. He was right—I felt great! Looking back, I'm so glad that I got out of the boat and plunged into that water. It would be the last time we skied together, but at least I have the memory.

A couple of months after Shaun died, my friend Pam recommended that I get a puppy. My initial thought was, How in the world can I take care of a puppy? I can't even get out of bed and take care of myself. After giving it some consideration, though, I decided to keep an open mind. Not knowing what type of dog I wanted, I learned about different breeds and sizes. I decided on a small dog and went to visit a litter that was for sale. They had some adorable puppies. When I saw a precious Shih Tzu-Chihuahua mix, I fell in love. It didn't take long to know that little girl was going home with us. We had a forty-five-minute drive, so I nestled her inside my warm coat, and the bond between us was instantaneous. She became my grief dog and helped ease some of my anguish. Even getting up at night with her was good for me—somebody else's needs were more pressing than mine. Adorable, soft, and so playful, little Sami helped the entire family.

One day, as I was leaving the house, she looked at me with those big, pleading eyes and I couldn't bear to leave her alone. Right away, I started looking for another puppy so she would have a companion. A little Yorkie called Lexi was the next member of our family. She was so tiny, she fit on the keyboard of a laptop. Sensitive and sweet, Lexi was loved by us all. Now we had two tiny puppies and two large dogs that Shaun had left behind— Ice and Kennan. The big ones loved the puppies too, even though at times they were jealous of the attention the two little ones received.

Kevin had warned me when I went to look at the second puppy that I'd better not bring her home. He loved dogs, but he thought four was too many. When I did, he wasn't happy and told me they were my responsibility. I did everything for those puppies. Having them encouraged me to dig deep for the energy I needed to care for them. The cuddling and kisses they gave me, along with the happiness I saw the rest of the family experience, helped my heart to heal. Even Kevin came around and claimed Lexi as his dog. Now, our life revolves around these two little girls. We know they will leave us one day and there will be a void in our hearts, but neither of us would give up what we gained from them over these difficult years. Many times, I've suggested to other grieving parents that they get a pet. When you pour your love on an animal that needs you, a transformation occurs.

In spite of the lift the puppies gave me, I had yet to find the strength to go back to work. There was no room in my mind for thoughts of anything other than the son I could no longer be with. The loss of him filled up every part of me—I couldn't concentrate on anything else. I wanted to crawl into the crack of my heart and find him. I knew he was in there, if I could only get to him.

I kept reviewing in my mind the course of his life and all the beautiful attributes he had developed. Shaun's battle with cancer had inspired him to appreciate life and be all that he could be. He was patient, compassionate, and put others ahead of himself. When he started college, he worked a full-time job all summer and kept a part-time job during the school months. He liked having money and took pride in being independent. He rarely asked for help—in fact, I had to guess when he needed something. I had grown up the same way, believing in self-sufficiency, so I respected his pride. He had big plans for his life, and I didn't want him to get distracted and lose focus. I wanted him to understand the importance of working hard toward his goals and standing on his own feet. However, the college years were tough on him, and after his death, I wished I had helped him more.

Shaun dreamed of being a doctor and helping children who were sick with cancer. He wanted to be a doctor so much that he often said he wished he was already there. I told him, "Enjoy the ride, Shaun. It's the best part." But it wasn't Shaun who needed to hear those words—it was me! After Shaun died, I saw that I hadn't learned to live in the present. Everything I'd ever wanted had been right in front of me, but I was so busy working and trying to reach the next goal, I didn't see it. I'd achieve a milestone and already be thinking about my next step, forgetting to give myself time to appreciate where I was. My life had been perfect, but I was too blind to see it.

At night, as I struggled to fall asleep, I would bargain with God and beg him to send Shaun back to me one last time so we could at least say goodbye. I desperately wanted to know the reason why he had to leave us. I felt like I couldn't be at peace until I understood why he had died at this time and in this way. It was my new nighttime ritual—praying, questioning, and agonizing over never getting any answers— until I cried myself to sleep.

Although I didn't receive the answer to my questions, at times I felt Shaun's spiritual presence. During the first few weeks after his death, I could feel him shaking my heart. It's hard to describe, but it was as if his spirit was inside my body, causing my heart to vibrate. The sensation was real, and I knew it was him trying to tell me, "I'm here. I'm still with you, and I'm all right."

In spite of these comforting experiences, however, grief continued to overwhelm my life. All I wanted to do was withdraw from the world, to reach into my heart where Shaun dwelled, and hold him forever.

WHEN BY CINDY BAUMANN

When the wind swirls the snow up into the air,
I look for my son.
When the wind blows the trees,
I look for my son.
When a butterfly lands on a flower,
I look for my son.
When the clouds have a unique formation,
I look for my son.
When the air is still,
I look for my son.
When the lights in the house flicker,
I look for my son.
When the house feels silent,
I look for my son.
When the song on the radio speaks to me,
I look for my son.
When I see 1:11 or 11:11 on the clock,
I look for my son.
When the stars twinkle brightly,
I look for my son.
When the sunset is vibrant and beautiful,
I look for my son.
When I find a penny shining on the ground,
I look for my son.
When the night is hushed and quiet,
I look for my son.
I will forever look for my son . . .

CHAPTER NINE

EARTH ANGELS AT CHRISTMAS

My prayer: Mother Mary, you know the pain of losing a son.
Help me to survive the pain of losing mine on this day,
the birthday of your baby boy.

LESS THAN A month had gone by since Shaun died, and the Christmas holidays were around the corner. The absence of his enthusiasm and laughter surrounded us. How could we have Christmas without him? Each person in the family had always had their special place in the living room to sit while we opened our gifts. Every time I looked at Shaun's favorite spot in front of the entertainment center, the twisting pain in my chest grew heavier. That place would forever be his.

It was impossible for us to think about celebrating. I didn't want to decorate the house, and I had no energy to do the shopping. We had a tree, but no desire to put it up. All I could think about was how this would be the first of an endless string of holidays our family would spend without Shaun. I tried to open the many Christmas cards we received, but that only made things worse. I didn't want to see the words Merry Christmas, because in my house, it wasn't.

It seemed like everybody else's lives continued with happiness, while ours had ended abruptly on that cold November day. It bewildered me how the world continued around me like nothing had changed. Whenever

I looked out my window, I saw cars moving and people walking and going about their normal activities, but it was as if they were far away, nothing but an illusion. I felt as though I couldn't hear anything out in the world either, as if the glass on my window was a foot thick. I might as well have been watching the world turn from a different planet, and Christmas was no different.

A few days before Christmas, my husband and I were sitting at home with the kids and my parents, unable to muster the energy to do anything, when three angels—Randy, Roger, and Susan—appeared at our door with armfuls of Christmas decorations. Not only did they bring everything that was needed, but Randy, who owned a unique floral and gift shop, decorated the whole tree for us. I sat in awe as he transformed the fragrant pine into a beautiful work of art, perfectly adorned with thousands of white lights, stars, icicles, red and green twigs, and just the right number of ornaments. I had always admired the trees he decorated in his store, and now I had one standing in my living room. God bless my wonderful friends. They had planned the whole thing, knowing that my other kids needed a Christmas tree and understanding how hard it would be for us to make it happen this year. That evening was so special, and once again I felt Shaun's loving, grateful energy in the room with us.

Christmas Day arrived, and it was as hard as I'd expected. Knowing it was important for the rest of the family to gather, I tried my best to be strong. To help us all cope, we changed our routine. We didn't go to our normal Christmas Eve Mass or have prime rib, as was customary. Both sets of our parents showed up, knowing how much we needed them, and each brought a dish to share. Celebrating at home was hard enough, and then it was time to gather with my siblings, nieces, nephews, cousins, and Kevin's extended family as well. I didn't want to ruin everybody else's holiday, so I had to attend, but all I wanted to do was stay at home and curl up in bed. I went through the motions, but none of it felt real.

New Year's was a repeat of Christmas . . . relentless torture. People around us were setting new goals, moving ahead, and making plans for the future. Again, there was no "Happy New Year" in our house, no visions of hope for the future. I knew I had a lot to be grateful for and still had wonderful, loving people in my life, but in such a state of grief, I could not focus on what I had, only on what I had lost. The pain inside my heart consumed every part of me, and situations that would normally bring me joy only brought sadness. My days were dark and long. No matter how much I slept, I woke exhausted.

One day, Jordan asked, "Mom, when are you going back to work?"

I didn't know how to answer him, and I sensed his fear over my depression. I didn't blame him—he wondered if his mom was ever going to stop crying. Even though it was the last thing I wanted to do, I made the tough decision to go back to the office. Kevin and the kids were dealing with unrelenting grief, and I knew they needed this from me.

Work was as tough as I expected it to be. Frequently, I found myself facing the wall in my office, crying throughout the day. I was there physically, but I couldn't control my mind enough to focus on anything practical. All I could think about was going home to see if Shaun was there. I was tormented by a stream of intrusive thoughts: I need to go look for Shaun. I can't find him if I'm stuck at work all day. If he comes home and I'm not there, I might miss him if he has to go again. Maybe this is a nightmare. Please, God, wake me up! These ideas weren't logical, but they felt real at the time. No matter how hard I tried to shift my attention to the work at hand, I was preoccupied with Shaun returning home. The conflict I felt between my thoughts and the tasks I had to complete left me physically and mentally spent.

My coworkers had no idea how hard the days were for me. I could tell people were watching me for signs that I was pulling out of my despair. Most of them tried to ignore the subject; others were brave enough to ask me how I was doing. Very few seemed to expect an honest answer, and nobody knew how to handle me. I don't say this to criticize how people reacted to me. I understand that it's incredibly hard to know how to help somebody who is grieving. Most of us feel uncomfortable when discussing death or seeing somebody expressing such intense emotions.

My car took the brunt of my outbursts—it was where I felt I could express my feelings without the need to pretend. When I drove somewhere, I'd cry and beg Shaun to help me and give me answers about what had happened, but when I got no response, I would pray to God to help me find peace in my heart. I was afraid that I would never feel a moment of true joy again for the rest of my life.

The prospect of permanently feeling the way I did terrified me. Sometimes, I'd pull over to the side of the road when I was driving home and just sob. I wanted to let it all out before I got home, so I could pull myself together before I saw my family. There were times when people stopped alongside my car and asked if I was okay. When I told them, "I lost my son," I knew they felt awkward and wished they hadn't stopped. People wanted to help, but they didn't know how. How could they? There wasn't anything anybody could do for me—I just needed to let the tears flow. They seemed to cleanse my soul. Nothing felt good or brought me any release, but crying was sometimes better than not crying.

It was the simple things where I felt Shaun's absence that hit me the hardest. The first time I went to the grocery store after the loss, I had a meltdown in the peanut butter aisle. It was hard to walk by the foods my son loved. He appreciated his food, and it broke my heart to think that he would never eat these things again. Remembering his sweet tooth made the baking aisle difficult as well. I remember being in Walgreens and walking by the hair gel. Whenever I went shopping, Shaun would tell me to pick up a particular brand of gel for him, and it struck me that he would never ask me to do that again. The thought of this crushed me, and I slumped on the floor in Walgreens and wept. I never knew when these waves of overwhelming grief would hit me; the simplest thing could trigger a feeling of sorrow so deep, it brought me to my knees. I wore my sunglasses to the store so people wouldn't feel uncomfortable around me. Wherever I went, they were part of my wardrobe.

I remembered all the special things he did when he was alive—the calls, the texts, the conversations, the unexpected moments of tenderness. I missed just looking at him, watching him smile, and listening to the way he talked. There will always be days that are tougher than others: Mother's Day, his birthday, their wedding anniversary, Christmas, and of course the anniversary of his death which will forever be the worst day of my life.

It was the simple things I'd shared with Shaun that I missed the most . . . all those little things that go toward making big ones. Whenever we were cooking together in the kitchen, he would tease me, and I would give it right back.

He would ask, "What are you making for dinner, Mom?"

"Spaghetti. Are you interested? Oh, wait a minute, you are probably having chicken for the fifth time this week, right?"

"As a matter of fact, I am, but thanks for the offer, Mom."

He loved chicken and created his own recipes. In one, he coated the chicken breast in graham crackers and for health reasons, he baked it. It was pretty tasty and crunchy.

We both had a fun competitive streak and loved to tease each other about whose recipe was better or just about anything that would make the other smile, but it was all in jest. Our personalities were similar, and we weren't really out to win. I loved it when he called me Mom. I was so proud to be his mother. I remember looking at him at times and thinking, You bring so much joy to my life. I could tell he enjoyed my company too. It warmed my heart to know that the feeling was mutual.

Sometimes, we would sneak away to Starbucks, or we'd go shopping together. The conversation never lagged, and we always found something to laugh about. The phrase kindred spirits describe us. I never grew tired of being with him, whether it was working on a project together or just taking a walk outside. Shaun and I loved to spend time outdoors and bonded over our love of nature. He was determined to teach me how to run with more endurance, so we often ran up the hill near our house. The scenery there was magical. The trees made a canopy over the road, with sunshine dappling through the branches. There was always something beautiful to see, whether it was the deer we startled, the colorful fall leaves, or catching the sunset at the end of the trail. It was never just the two of us on the trails—we always brought the dogs along. He had a soft heart for his pets and would never leave them home when we could all be together.

Our home was in the woods on the edge of the city, and we spent hours walking or riding the four-wheeler along a dirt trail that ran through tall oaks and majestic pine trees. Sometimes, it seemed he just wanted to get me on the four-wheeler so we could spend time together, talking about whatever came to mind. He always pushed me to keep up with him, no matter what we were doing. He was a fit kid. He took good care of his body and worked out every day—and yet he thought his mom could do it all too.

I have no doubt this drive for health and strength came from what he'd endured as a child. He wanted to keep his body healthy, and he urged everybody around him to do the same. He inspired me to be my best in every area of my life. I will never forget those special times we shared in the beauty of nature; they will always be some of my most cherished memories. There was no part of my life where Shaun's absence wasn't felt.

Home wasn't home anymore; it was just a house. Shaun was everywhere I looked, and yet, he was nowhere. His empty chair haunted me. It was unbearable. I wanted a fresh start where the loss of his presence didn't occupy every space. Not everybody reacts this way to death. Some people never want to move away from their house. They want to hold onto the memories by keeping things just as they were. Others, like me, need to change their environment. There's no right or wrong when it comes to making this decision. However, with the state of the economy, we couldn't sell our house, and as a result, I felt trapped, both outwardly and in the physical sense, to a location and a state of mind that I couldn't escape.

It wasn't just me who learned from Shaun and loved him deeply—he touched the lives of all his friends in a special way. He cared about what was going on in their lives, and they knew it. Some of his close friends—Bryce, Greg, Matt, and Laine—and his nieces, nephews, cousins, and brother-in-law all admired him, and after his passing, looked for ways to keep him with them. His cousin Tate had Shaun's initials, SLW, tattooed on his side. Whitney, another cousin, had a special symbol tattooed on her neck, and his brother-in-law David had WWSD—What Would Shaun Do— tattooed on the inside of his wrist. They all wanted Shaun to know how much they valued what he'd taught them and to honor him as they could.

Julia's family grieved deeply for Shaun. They'd all loved him—he was the kind of person people admired and didn't forget. It hurt me to imagine what Julia was going through, but then I didn't have to imagine it because I was going through it too. My thoughts often turned to their beautiful wedding day. You could feel the love in the air; what they had was the real deal. I knew my son would have a strong, happy marriage. It strengthened them and made everybody around them believe in love. When they got engaged, Shaun wrote in the sand on the beach I Will Love You Forever and buried the engagement ring for Julia to find. Leave it to my son to think of such a romantic, fun way to surprise his soul mate. Their invitations to the wedding and many of their gifts referenced the words he'd written in the sand. We knew they would love each other forever, or in their case, it was "until death do us part."

> *Journal Entry*
> *February 6, 2008*
> *Dear Shaun,*
>
> *I apologize for not writing as often. I have been busy reading lots of books, so I can try and understand my life without you physically present. I'm trying, Shaun. Please lead me to the right people who will have compassion and understanding while I sort things out. I'm asking you to guide me. Perhaps I should be doing something else with my life. Today,*

St. Matt's had a Mass for you and, as you know, it's Ash Wednesday. The church is still very emotional for me.

I know I'm getting greedy, but I would like you to turn my angels on at least a couple of times a week. I feel a closeness when they are on. I miss you, Shaun. Please try and hug me every day. How do you like Samantha, the new little addition to our family? Isn't she just the sweetest little puppy? She brings a long-lost smile to our faces. Please play with her while I'm at work.

Shaun, I would like you to visit me in my dreams. Please come to me and spend time with me like you did before. Make me laugh. Tell me about your new life. I love you, Shaun, and I still wish God hadn't taken you from us.

XXXO Mom

P.S. Have you seen Tate's tattoo? I love seeing your initials: S.L.W.

CHAPTER TEN

GRIEF: MIND AND BODY

I looked in the mirror today and I didn't know who I was anymore.
—*Cindy Baumann*

GRIEF DEVASTATED MY mind and emotions, but it affected my body as well. Shortly after Shaun passed, I developed a sensation of tightness around my throat and chest. It felt like something was putting pressure on my heart, and I found it hard to breathe. Sometimes, I literally had to remind myself to take a breath. I'd been taking an anxiety medication prescribed by my doctor for three months, and now he wanted to add on something for depression. I was so eager for something to make me feel better, I took everything he prescribed faithfully, but to my disappointment, my suffering didn't go away.

Desperate to find some kind of relief, I attended a grief support group, but as soon as I opened the door to the room, my heart sank to the floor. I knew this wasn't the place for me. My throat closed and my chest tightened. I had to force myself to take a breath before stepping inside. The place was filled with parents who had lost their children. There were pictures on the bulletin board of their young, beautiful faces. It was a room filled with a deep, aching sadness, the kind of sadness I knew all too well.

The meeting opened with everybody going around the room, telling their stories, one tragic experience after another. Their stories were heart-wrenching, people who had lost their children ten years earlier could hardly get through their story without breaking down. I saw my future in those parents . . . nothing but sorrow lay ahead, even many years from now. I couldn't handle my grief, let alone everybody's in the room. I was looking for hope, not more pain. I couldn't fully feel their pain since mine was so all-consuming. There was no space left inside me to take on anyone else's. I wanted to crawl under the table before it was my turn. As I walked to my car that night, I prayed I could find another way to survive the darkness. If not, I didn't know if I could make it.

Although this group wasn't right for me, I knew I needed to keep searching for something to ease my desperation. Fortunately, I found Wings, a grief education ministry program developed by a husband-and-wife team, Nan and Gary, after they lost their son to suicide. Nan explained the program to me and encouraged me to give it a try. As I drove to the session, I wondered if it was going to be similar to the last one I'd attended. It was held at a hospital, and as I walked in, memories of the last time I touched Shaun's face hit me hard. I could see him lying on that bed in the hospital room, his beautiful eyes closed forever, and the chill of death ran through my body. With each step I took toward the meeting room, my anxiety increased, and I began struggling to breathe. It took all my strength to open the door and enter, but a friend was attending, so I felt compelled to go to at least one session.

We sat around a large sterile table, and I choked out my story. We were handed a packet, a book, and an agenda which outlined the program. I tried to take a breath as I opened the book and scanned the list of topics: shock, depression, denial, anger, and more. Understanding the components of grief was something I needed to learn more about, so I stuck with it. Over time, Nan, Gary, and the group brought hope into my life. It helped to know I wasn't navigating this by myself. I was grateful for their support.

Along with the anxiety, I went through other physical reactions to grief as well. During the first six months after Shaun died, I perspired so profusely that I had to change my clothes and sometimes even the sheets several times a night. My doctor was concerned, so he checked me for lymphoma since heavy sweating is a symptom of the condition. I wasn't too concerned about the possibility of having cancer. At that point, I didn't care if I lived or died. The grief was unbearable; I figured if heaven was such a great place, I was ready to go.

When the test came back negative for lymphoma, we assumed I must be in menopause, even though I was younger than what was considered typical. My doctor said the trauma might have thrown me into early menopause, but a year later when he tested my hormone levels, we found out that wasn't the case. He concluded that my body had been trying to shut down due to the emotional stress I was under. He said he had never seen anything like it, but it was the only explanation he could come up with.

On top of my physical struggles, I also lost the comfort I'd found in the church. As much as I wanted to search for solace there, it had the opposite effect. The music and Scriptures reminded me of Shaun's funeral, and when the service referred to the "communion of saints" and "remembering loved ones who had gone before us," all I could think of was how far away Shaun was from me. I distanced myself from the church and went less often with every passing month. I was angry with God, but that's not the only reason I didn't want to go. If Jesus could rise from the dead, why couldn't Shaun? He had lived a good life. Like Christ, he had suffered yet went on to be a loving influence on everybody he had come across. And what about the teaching "He will come again?" All my life I was afraid of Christ coming again. Now, I was ready for his return when he would unite us with our loved ones. I couldn't wait. If Shaun couldn't come to me, I was ready to go to him. I didn't want to be here.

As life continued, I had little choice but to continue with it. Spring rolled around, a season symbolic of renewal, but I stayed stuck in the same place. As the leaves turned a beautiful bright shade of green, I was reminded of how much Shaun loved the outdoors. The calendar kept moving, but I couldn't. One day I'd be wondering why Shaun wasn't home, and the very next day I'd be questioning why he didn't visit me in spirit. I'd felt his presence before, and felt certain he'd turned on the angel light in my bedroom more than once, but I needed more from him. I believed he could reach out if he wanted to, and I was angry with him for not trying.

Six months passed, and the month of May was approaching. I anticipated and feared Mother's Day. I was still a mother, but I didn't feel whole anymore. The missing piece from my heart kept pulling on me, like scar tissue that constantly reminds you of an area of your body that is damaged. This was one of the hardest days to get through. I didn't want anybody to wish me, "Happy Mother's Day." I couldn't even wish my mother a happy day. I just wanted it to come and go without any mention. I thought back to all the sweet messages Shaun had included in the cards he gave me. I almost expected him to find a way to slip a card into the mailbox to tell me he was thinking of me and life was good where he was. This day was important. He knew that. Surely it wouldn't come and go without him contacting me in some way. Sadly, it did and I felt forgotten.

Summer arrived, Shaun's favorite season, but this year the sunshine did anything but make us smile. It was a standing tradition that in June Kevin and the boys went fishing in Canada. Shaun had always looked forward to spending quality time with his brothers and stepfather. This year, there was no Shaun, and I couldn't comprehend how they could think of going without him. They packed up their fishing gear and left me for ten days. I understand now that they wanted to show their support of each other as they tried to move on in life. They were also trying to honor Shaun's memory by upholding a tradition he loved, but at the time, I didn't see it that way. It seemed to me they were betraying him. I was hurt and confused by their leaving.

Those ten days were so hard on me. I was lonely and missed them. In addition, I'd developed an exaggerated fear for the safety of my other boys, so I constantly imagined the worst. I knew I'd never survive another loss and worried about one of them being taken from me. The hours ticked by, my heart pounding and my anxiety through the roof. As it was, when they returned from the trip, I was horrified to hear that Jordan, who was driving, had swerved to miss a tree in the road and totaled the truck. One of their friends was hospitalized for several days. The rest of them were bruised, sore, and had a few cuts, but they were all okay. I had a feeling that Shaun was there protecting them in that moment.

No matter where I turned, I found no relief from my fear and sadness, and I turned to thoughts of suicide. This may sound extreme, especially as I had other children who I loved dearly, but after I lost Shaun, just living and breathing on this planet was a torment. I was tired . . . so incredibly tired of going through the daily motions of life, and I believed my family would be better off if they didn't have to see me in this state of mind.

In the past, I'd had a fear of dying because I never wanted to be separated from my family, but after I lost Shaun, that fear left me. I trusted that a loving God would accept me despite my shortcomings and reunite me with Shaun. Sometimes, I sat at work after everybody had left for the day and looked at my wrists. I had great veins and they were close to the surface—they taunted and dared me. I thought it would be quick and easy to cut them. In a matter of minutes, I could be gone from this awful world before anybody found me. I envisioned myself lying on the floor in my office with blood seeping into the carpet and life slipping away from me.

The same cold feeling came over me that I felt when I last touched Shaun, yet there was something peaceful about it. I imagined him reaching out his hand to help me cross over. I wanted to grab it and be liberated from this earth. In the evening, I would lie in the bathtub and think about grabbing the handles and holding myself underwater. I wondered how long it would take to drown myself. I thought it might be impossible to hold myself under the water long enough. I plotted several ways to end my suffering. If heaven was such a great place, and Shaun was already there, I wanted to join him.

After considering suicide several times, I decided I couldn't do it to my family. How would my other children feel if I took my life? I knew they couldn't comprehend the state of sadness I was in and the energy it took to stay alive each day. If I died, they would think I loved them less, though nothing could be further from the truth—I didn't want to be separated from them any more than I wanted to be separated from Shaun. The last thing I wanted was for them to feel the kind of agony I was feeling, but in truth they were already experiencing just that. Not only were they heartbroken over Shaun, but also over the condition I was in. I was just too immersed in my grief to realize it.

I decided that I had to find a way to live and stop running from the painful feelings inside. It was pointless anyway, because they always seemed to catch me. I tried to reason with myself, reversing the situation and asking myself how I would have wanted Shaun to feel if I had died in an accident. I knew I would do everything I could to relieve him of that guilt. His happiness would be all I cared about. Looking at things this way made me see that I wasn't helpless and unable to reach Shaun. Even though we lived in different dimensions, I had something valuable to give him—my happiness.

Somebody told me that living had to start with forgiving myself before I could recover from my loss. They said I should forgive the two men involved with the shooting—the one who set up the deer drive and the one who pulled the trigger. Do I feel they intentionally put Shaun in harm's way? No. I know in my heart that his death was an accident. Nobody planned to kill Shaun, and I'm certain they live with their own piece of hell whenever they think about the young man who died because of their actions. But the plain facts were that somebody took my son's life and I was angry with them.

For years, I waited for a letter from the shooter and the person who set up the deer drive. I wanted them to come to me with an apology, but it never came. I concluded that neither could find any words to do the situation justice. I tried to let it go, but I still wonder if I'll get a letter someday.

I felt my forgiveness would give Shaun the greatest peace, and I truly wanted to give it to him, but the hurt was too deep. I knew he wanted this, not only for the shooter, but for all of us. I'd read so much about forgiveness and how holding onto resentment is damaging on so many levels. I wanted to take that step, but it was a complicated process. It took a long time for me to be ready to forgive.

To distract myself from the constant pain I was in, I ventured out into creative projects. Engaging in them provided me with company without requiring me to socialize with people. I found many things I could do while alone and release some of what I had churning inside me. My first choice was photography. I'd seen so much horror that now something in me wanted to capture whatever beauty I could find. I'd wake up early to catch the sunrise and then walk to one of Shaun's favorite places to take a photograph. The camera opened my eyes to how much magic there is in our world. I became absorbed in the gorgeous colors, shapes and scents of the flowers, sky, landscapes, and hills.

As my photography improved, I began to share some of my visuals through note cards and pictures for others. The more time I spent in nature, the more I realized that I had the opportunity to focus on either the beauty of life or the ugliness of it. Both extremes were available to me at all times. It was up to me to choose. When I picked beauty, I felt connected to the heavenly realm where Shaun lives. When I picked ugliness, I became immersed in the misery of loss.

Next, I turned to making jewelry, and then I took up knitting. My concentration was limited, so I kept my projects short and easy. Needless to say, I made lots of scarves. They became my new perfect Christmas gift for my sisters. Creativity was good for my soul. It gave my heart a break, especially working with the life-giving energy of color. I often cried through my projects, but it made me feel good inside to use my time and energy to make something beautiful in this world. Whenever my family was out of the house or away on a trip, creating calmed my mind and stopped me from obsessing about what could happen.

In the middle of summer, in keeping with our family's tradition, we headed north to our cabin for the weekend. The cabin was a haven in Northern Wisconsin where the work ended and play took over. It was a place where we could come together, leave our cares behind, and enjoy a variety of activities. To Shaun, it had been a piece of paradise, his favorite spot in all the world. He loved everything about it and claimed it as his own. He and Julia had even spent a summer living at the cabin while he worked construction and she taught school in the area. I remember telling him that would be one of the best summers of his life, and from what I saw, it really was. I didn't know it would be his last.

I knew it would be hard for us to go there, and it was. Everywhere we turned, we felt both the absence and presence of Shaun. I had to sit on the beach where he wrote words in the sand to Julia, and we had to walk past the bedroom he'd shared with her. His ski, vest, and wetsuit hung in the entryway; I put them away so that nobody else would use them. It was a full house, with Ryan, Maria, Jordan, Justin, Kevin, and I there—and yet it was an empty house without Shaun. I spent hours sitting on the dock, staring over the calm water at the horizon, sobbing. I wanted to go back to the year before, when life was perfect.

Every Sunday, my parents would join us, both to offer support and to ease their own pain. They'd suffered terribly over the loss of the grandson they'd loved so dearly. They'd always been close to all their grandchildren, but Ryan and Shaun had received special attention in the early years. They had taken care of Ryan while I was at the hospital with Shaun, and they'd poured their love onto Shaun, praying that God would heal him.

I remember how when Shaun finished his chemotherapy treatments, they took us to Disney World. This was a dream come true for the boys. They'd never had the chance to experience any excitement in their young lives. Fran and I were poor, and in our little town there was nothing like that around us. Even if there had been, we wouldn't have gone, because we had to keep ourselves isolated to protect Shaun's immune system through-out his cancer treatments.

When the boys first entered Disney World, they were overjoyed. They truly believed it was a fantasy land. We went on rides and got lots of hugs from the characters. They even watched as Shamu jumped out of the water and kissed me at Sea World. Yes, it was a real Kodak moment! We also went to Busch Gardens and went shelling on Cocoa Beach. I would give anything to go back and experience those days again with my two little boys and my parents. It is one of my favorite memories.

When Shaun died, it broke my parents' hearts. Seeing my level of depression, they were afraid they'd lose me too. As much as they hurt, they tried to hold it together, grieving in silence most of the time. I saw the sadness in their eyes, and witnessed my dad cry for the first time. Their faith was strong, however, and they prayed to God to help our family. I know it bothered my mother that I quit going to church. For a woman that never misses Mass, I'm sure it was difficult seeing her daughter's loss of faith, but she never said anything to pressure me.

Despite everyone's efforts to help each other that summer, a silence hung over the cabin, and we didn't know what to do with ourselves. In the past, the ski boat would run continuously. This year, we didn't take it off the lift until the middle of July and didn't go skiing until August. Our motivation was gone, but we forced ourselves into the water. If we could make one run, we would be satisfied.

Kevin went first. I knew it was going to be tough for him because Shaun was his main ski buddy. Justin went next, and then I took my turn. When I grabbed the handle of the ski rope, I didn't think I would have the strength to get up on my ski, but Shaun must have given me a boost. I managed to rise up, and with the water splashing on my face, the tears fell. As I skied around the lake, I thought of our last run together a year ago and felt my heart break all over again. It took everything I had to stay up on my ski, but I did—in honor of him.

After that first summer, I wanted to focus on something other than memories of Shaun, as precious as they were, so we made the gut-wrenching decision to put the cabin up for sale. Our kids loved the cabin, and it was filled with so many happy memories. I was torn between holding on to those moments and running away from them. I thought it was easier to run. I have wondered since if it was a selfish decision, but it was all I could do at the time.

As it was, Shaun was up to mischief again, because it took us four years to sell it. I guess he wanted to know that we were completely sure. As hard as it was to go back to the cabin during those years, it gave me time to face the depth of my grief, something that's essential for recovery, and it let the kids adjust to the idea of letting go of our vacation spot. When it finally sold, it was a bittersweet day, to say the least.

CHAPTER ELEVEN

PUSHING THROUGH

I'm lost at sea without a compass to navigate back.
—*Cindy Baumann*

WE CONTINUED TO push through the milestones of that first year without Shaun. When what would have been his first wedding anniversary arrived, I was faced with another layer of sorrow. A year ago, we'd all anticipated a future filled with many wedding anniversaries and family gatherings. The cake top that Shaun and Julia should have enjoyed on their first anniversary was still in my freezer, and I didn't know what to do with it. One of the happiest days of our lives was now one of the saddest.

I loved Julia and her family, and not seeing them regularly anymore added to the sense of loss. Their kindness and warmth had added a sense of completeness to my life, and now that was gone as well. Julia was still in Madison. but had moved out of the home she had shared with Shaun into her girlfriend's apartment. She couldn't go back to the place where she'd lost her heart. She stopped coming as often to her parents' house in Wausau too. We all understood, of course, but it didn't make us miss her any less. This was the city where she had met and fallen in love with Shaun, then lost him after only three months of marriage. My heart ached for her. I yearned to take her sadness away and bring back her beautiful smile. I couldn't imagine how hard it was on her, knowing they would never have a baby together, a part of him to live on. Sometimes I would dream of their children. I had no doubt Shaun and Julia would've passed all their wonderful traits onto their kids. And, best of all, they'd have called me Grandma.

On September 8 at 7:38 a.m., I suddenly woke up and stared at my clock. My inner alarm had told me it was the exact time Shaun had been born. I wondered if from heaven he could feel any connection to his earthly birthday. As I lay in bed, I prayed that he was safe and at peace and that he could feel how much we appreciated, loved, and missed him. I tried to be strong but ended up spending the rest of the day in bed, crying most of the time. It was inconceivable to me that after twenty-seven years, this was the first time I couldn't wish him a happy birthday.

Birthdays had always been special in our home, but today, there was nothing to celebrate. I missed my little boy so very much. I was a good mother to Shaun—why would God take him away from me? I knew his birthday would be tough, but I never anticipated the level of sadness I felt or the utter desolation that overwhelmed me. I was a hollow shell.

As November approached, bringing with it "the worst day of my life," I thought about what I could do to avoid the anguish I'd felt throughout the last year. We were nearly through all the "firsts" of the year without Shaun, and I wanted to do something positive—something Shaun would be proud of. I arranged to visit some foundations in order to learn more about how to strengthen the scholarship our friends had set up when Shaun died. The Shaun L. Winter Memorial Scholarship was awarded to one student every year who was transferring to the University of Wisconsin–Madison in the medical field.

I'm so glad I chose to spend the day of Shaun's passing in such a way. I resisted the urge to-stay in bed and left the house on a mission to make a difference. I had hoped if I could do one thing to help somebody else, the day would be better, and I was right. It was something Shaun would've wanted me to do. The scholarship stands today as a tribute to his generous heart. I'll forever be grateful to all our friends and family who contributed and continue to donate to the scholarship (https://greatstartswithu.org/where-to-give/endowed-scholarship-fund/).

I had read that the first year after someone dies is the hardest and hoped that would be the case as we moved away from that year of painful firsts. I honestly couldn't believe we had survived this long without him, and I prayed the second year would be better. However, I found that as the shock of his death wore off, the harsh reality of him never coming back increased. It felt like the current of time was pulling me further and further away from him. I was afraid that as I got older, I might start to forget things about our life together. I knew no matter how many years passed, I would feel the same love for him to the moment of my last breath and beyond, but what about him? I didn't know if he would still remember me and love me the same way as time went by.

Each night, I went to bed and woke up exhausted. Finally, I addressed the fact that I had not slept through the night in over a year, and my doctor prescribed a sleeping aid. To my great relief, I got some regular sleep at last. Once I had the sleeping down, it was the waking that scared me the most. Every morning, I would open my eyes, and within seconds I'd remember what I'd lost. Those few seconds before reality hit were the only moments in the day when I was free of grief. I would hope it was a terrible nightmare, but had to face that it wasn't. I was stuck in the same thought patterns, an endless loop of sadness, denial, and confusion. Every day was like Ground Hog Day.

The second year is the time when everybody else expects you to get better. I sensed the pressure on me to get back to my normal, busy life, but I wasn't ready. Everybody grieves differently. Some people throw themselves into as many activities as they can, and others do the opposite. In my case, I just wanted to stay home, sit on the couch in the living room in front of the big picture window, and stare into the sky. When I was little and lost an animal, my mom told me to watch for it in the cloud formations. I would look for hours to find my pets. It seemed so surreal to be staring into the sky watching for an image of my son to float by. I also thought if I would just sit home alone in silence, I might hear him speak to me.

I'd always been a social butterfly, but now my social life was non-existent. After turning down the invitations of our friends several times, they quit asking us out. It wasn't that I felt I shouldn't have a good time—I just couldn't do it. I didn't want to either. At home, I didn't have to pretend to anybody that I was all right. There was no need for faking or struggling to stay focused on their conversations or the trivia of their daily life. I wasn't interested in anything they had to say. My life wasn't important to me, so how could I possibly care about theirs? At home, I could be myself.

At the urging of others, I decided to take a photography class at the university to sharpen my skills. At first, it sounded like a good idea. After all, I had seen how things could vanish, and I wanted to immortalize them.

But I hadn't thought about the feelings I'd have when I walked into the same college Shaun had attended a few years earlier. The first night in class, my mind followed Shaun's steps through the school. It felt like he should be walking through the hallways, sitting in the chair, and listening to the lecture.

I was tormented with questions about him. What were his classes like? Which ones did he love the most? Was I sitting in a chair he'd once sat in? Had his hand touched this doorknob? Was there a part of him still here in this place? I yearned to know every detail of what he'd done there. I'd never been heavily involved in his college life— he didn't need me to be. He was independent and did well in school. This was his school—not mine. He should be here instead of me.

On my way home from the photography class, my emotions took over. Trying to see through the tears was like trying to see through a hard rain without windshield wipers, and I had to pull over to the side of the road. I was a mile from home, and I couldn't get there. The tears turned into a state of panic. I was crying so hard I couldn't breathe. Thinking I might pass out, I cupped my hands over my mouth to try and slow my breathing. At that moment, it felt like I'd never be able to stop crying and gasping for air.

In desperation, I called my mother and cried out, "I can't live like this. I miss him too much. How do I go on? I don't have the strength."

My poor mother. She didn't know what to do for me, and yet she tried to be strong. She was fighting her own battle over losing her grandson, but at times like these, she always tried to comfort me. Every time I picked up the phone to call her, I hoped she could magically take the pain away like she did when I was a kid, bandaging my scraped knee after I had fallen from my bike. I knew there was no way she could make it all better, but she was always my first call. As time went on, I reached out less to her. It just wasn't fair to put her through it again and again. I knew she was there for me, but I didn't want to cause her more stress. Some things are so inexpressibly deep you can't share them, no matter how much you want to.

Grief triggers were everywhere, and there seemed to be no escape. My mind swayed between remembering the past and imagining what Shaun's future might have been like. He had reached the point in his life where his goals and dreams were unfolding. We had both been cheated . . . Shaun out of his career, marriage, and children and me out of the joy of participating in those things with him.

Work provided no distraction from my thoughts of Shaun either. When I was at my desk, I imagined him sitting across from me on the black cushioned guest chair in my office holding a smoothie he'd brought me for lunch. He had often stopped by my office, and now I missed those impromptu visits terribly. The grin on his face would instantly melt my heart and his presence lit up my day, even when he'd only pop in for a few minutes.

He'd once done a remodeling project for our office, and I wished I'd stopped working for a while and just watched him while he worked. I'd have given anything to see him swing his hammer or lift his paintbrush, but I was always so busy. Now, I regretted it. I wished I would have just paused for a few moments in my crazy day.

Time went on like this, with memories of the things I'd taken for granted causing me the greatest hurt. My grief was mixed with intense guilt and anger, and there seemed to be no end in sight. I went to my counseling appointments and kept myself involved with work and hobbies as best I could, and while some days were better than others, I still struggled far more than I let anyone know. I had a long, long way to go.

Journal Entry
February 14, 2009

It's Valentine's Day and I sure do miss you. At times, I can still feel you shaking my heart a bit. Last night I had a dream that you came home. I was so happy and hugged you so tight.

Love you,
Mom

Journal Entry
May 8, 2009

Last night, I had a dream that you appeared. I knew you were supposed to be dead. I asked you the same question I scream in the car when I'm alone, "Why did you have to leave us, Shaun?"

You held my hand and said, "And miss an opportunity for heaven? It had to be this way. I had to go."

Was that you, Shaun? Were you trying to tell me you were in heaven and that you are okay? This Earth is so hard!

Love you,
Mom

CHAPTER TWELVE

MORE ROUGH WATERS

*It hurts because the story of your life had so many more beautiful
chapters to it, but the book of your life had been abruptly closed.*
—*Narin Grewal*

KEVIN AND I got married when Shaun was nine and Ryan ten, and
they had a wonderful relationship. Ryan made Kevin work a little harder at
it, but that was understandable. The boys had been through a lot, shuttled
between my home and their dad's. I was happy to see them bond with Kevin the way they did. Their lives were enriched by this loyal and loving man.

Now that Shaun was gone, our family dynamics changed. I remembered how Shaun's years of illness had strained my first marriage to a
breaking point, and I feared what could happen between Kevin and me.
Granted, there were other factors involved, but not staying close to each
other while caring for a baby with cancer was at the root of our struggles. I
could feel the loss of Shaun affecting our relationship, day by day.

For the first year, Kevin and I just existed side by side in the house,
physically present but living inside our own worlds of grief. We each dealt
with it differently—Kevin found projects to keep him busy while I was
searching for another book to read, hoping to find something that would
bring me closer to Shaun. We were drowning in deep despair, and neither

of us had a life rope we could throw to the other. Grief grew, brick by brick, until there was a wall between us.

My therapist, Rick, told us how high the odds of divorce were in couples who had endured a loss like ours, and recommended marriage counseling. He explained how in times of grief people either turn toward each other for comfort, or they close their hearts and turn away, not because they don't care but because it's the only way they know to cope. Kevin and I didn't want to end up another statistic. We had to face what was going on between us, so we began meeting with Rick. Once again, this wonderful man was of tremendous help to us. He helped us revisit what had brought us together in the first place eighteen years ago.

He suggested that we read the book The Five Love Languages: The Secret to Love that Lasts by Gary Chapman. The premise of the book is that we all recognize and receive love in five main ways: words of affirmation, quality time, receiving gifts, acts of service, and physical touch. When we learn to speak our partner's love language, we are able to make them feel our love more fully. We saw that at this stage, neither of us was fulfilling the other's needs. Kevin and I started listening to each other and changed some things about how we related, staying mindful of what the other person required to feel valued and appreciated. Against the odds, we weathered the most terrible of storms and recently we celebrated our thirty-first anniversary. If you find that your relationship is crumbling under the weight of grief, I recommend professional help. It truly saved our marriage.

While I clung to things that had belonged to Shaun, Julia's way of grieving was different. She needed to see fewer of Shaun's personal belongings to cope. Little by little, she started bringing some of Shaun's things home to me. First, there was his wallet filled with pictures, and next his deodorant, toothbrushes, shaving cream, and other toiletries. Then she gave me some furniture he had made. There was a beautiful wood and marble table as well as their bed, which was made from stainless steel and wood. Among all his talents, Shaun was an accomplished carpenter, and his artistry showed in his handiwork. I wanted to find a place for everything, even if we didn't have space. These objects were precious to me. Of course, I didn't really want all his things back—I wanted him—but these things were all that was left.

I was approaching the end of the second year of Shaun's passing when I went for a routine mammogram. When the doctor told me an abnormality was noted in my right breast, I felt numb rather than shocked. After all that had happened so far in my life, I guess I had begun to expect the challenges to keep on coming. I had a biopsy, and on October 1, the first day of Breast Cancer Awareness Month, I learned that I had cancer.

I got the call at work and had to sit down to absorb it. A million thoughts rushed through my head: Oh good, I've wished for this. Now, maybe I can die and be free of the misery. I hope I don't have to suffer too much . . . maybe I have already paid that price. But what about my boys? They just lost their brother and now they could lose their mother. I want to live for them—or do I? Am I any use to them anymore, or just a burden? The most pressing thought of all, however, was, Does this mean I'll be with Shaun soon?

For most people, this diagnosis would have been devastating, but to me, cancer was so minor in the big picture. Still, the tears flowed, more for my family than for myself. Before I went home, I made sure I was all cried out. I wanted to be calm when I told the boys so I could make it sound less of a big deal. I called Kevin from work and told him first, asking him not to tell the boys yet. I felt the fear in his voice when he spoke—cancer was a death sentence in his mind.

As I walked in the door, Jordan and Justin, who were now eighteen and sixteen, could tell something was wrong. The look in their eyes was heartbreaking as they asked if everything was okay. Their lives had been turned upside down two years earlier, and they saw the world differently—it was a place where bad things could happen. When I told them that I'd received a call from my doctor and that I had cancer, they couldn't even look me in the eyes. Jordan looked away and Justin looked down at the counter. Fear was all over their innocent faces.

I downplayed the severity of it, saying they had caught it early and I would be all right. They seemed to accept what I said as the truth and, to my relief, didn't ask too many questions. It appeared I had calmed their fears, but I wondered if they were actually afraid to show their true feelings in front of me. Would this be one more thing they would take to their room and cry about in private?

For my cancer care, I chose the same healthcare system Shaun had gone to as a baby: Marshfield Clinic and St. Joseph's Hospital. Walking the familiar halls brought up a lot of tough memories for me. We had traveled to that hospital too many times to count throughout Shaun's life, starting with his childhood treatments and surgeries and followed by yearly check-ups to monitor the long-term effects of the radiation and chemo he had received. Those yearly visits were a time of anxiety for us all. Sometimes, it felt like we were living under the pendulum of death.

Now, just two years after Shaun's death, I was going to be making those same dreaded trips to Marshfield Clinic. Despite the disturbing memories I associated with the place, I trusted the doctors there and was grateful to them for saving my baby's life. I knew it was the best hospital for me to receive treatment for my cancer, so I sucked it up and began the series of required tests and exams.

One day, as I was driving home after an appointment, my mind churning with all the details the doctors had given me, I cried out to Shaun. "Where are you? I need you with me to get through this."

Immediately, I heard a voice in my mind say as clear as day, "Blue horse."

Blue horse? What's that supposed to mean? I thought. I was bewildered by the odd phrase randomly popping into my head, but as I rounded the bend, I was met with a big surprise—there was a house with a brilliant cobalt blue tin roof.

I had traveled this road hundreds of times before and had never seen this unusual roof. I knew right away Shaun was saying "blue house," not "blue horse." The sign was undeniable. He had given me something that would stand out and leave me with no doubt. He was validating that he was present during my ride home from the clinic.

Many more tests and appointments followed in the coming days, all in rapid succession. As I sat in the waiting room to see the oncologist, I found myself reading the cancer pamphlets. The more I read, the more I felt like an intruder had invaded my body, and I wanted it out of me. I wondered if I had manifested this illness as a way to leave this world. I felt death pressing in on one side and life on the other, and I knew I had a foot in both worlds. If I chose to, I could allow this cancer to take me out as easily as I could fight it. For the first time since hearing I had cancer, I became scared.

After the doctor completed his examination, he asked me some questions about my life. In his opinion, the trauma of Shaun's death was a contributor to my disease. Stress has a powerful effect on the immune system that can break down the body in some ways. I guess I was long overdue. I had a tumor in my chest, just like Shaun had as a baby, and it was in the spot where my heart ached constantly with grief. Not only that, it was near the area of the chest where Shaun had been shot. The symbolism and irony of these facts were not lost on me.

The radiologist requested another ultrasound of the area to make sure it wasn't larger than they'd thought. An MRI was scheduled, and the results frightened me more. By October 5, it was confirmed that this was the case. The doctor wanted to take a conservative approach, proceeding with a lumpectomy rather than doing a mastectomy right away, followed by radiation. Both of these treatments scared the hell out of me for different reasons. If I had a lumpectomy, the chances of a reoccurrence were greater than with a mastectomy, but hitting me with high doses of radiation made me nervous. What would the potential long-term side effects of that choice be—another cancer down the road?

The radiologist also saw a spot on the other breast but said she didn't think it was anything to worry about—yet. Since it was so deep, it was riskier to biopsy, and she was wary of inserting a wire that close to the proximity of my heart and lung. She suggested that we repeat the MRI on that side in six months, so we left that problem to deal with later and addressed the pending lumpectomy. Surgery was set for a few days later, and I was nervous about the wire guides they'd have to put into my breast before the operation. The idea of wires penetrating my breast tissue was horrifying. I wished they could put me to sleep for that part of the preparation, but that wasn't an option.

I was wheeled into the room expecting to see a biopsy table, but I was put in the mammography machine again. My breast was black and blue and filled with knots from the previous biopsies, but there was no way around it. It had to be compressed in the machine again. It was a traumatic and painful experience. They disinfected the area, and the smell of alcohol filled the room. A numbing agent was injected into my breast. I was already tender from all the testing and needles, so this just about put me over the edge. After taking several films, the radiologist inserted the first wire guide, which was thicker than I expected. It took three people to hold me in position for the procedure, and the cumulative effect of it got the better of me—I felt dizzy and hot despite the fan blowing on me.

I remember the tech saying, "Don't shut your eyes, Cindy."

I did everything in my power to remain calm and follow their directions, but nausea overwhelmed me, and I warned them, "I'm going to go."

I passed out with my breast compressed in the machine, and the radiologist's voice ringing in my ears: "Get a bed. Now."

They placed cool washcloths on my face, and I came to as they were trying to get me on to the bed without bumping the wire guides sticking out of my breast. They let me rest a short while, knowing the wiring process had to be finished. I felt Shaun saying, "You can do this, Mom."

I said, "Let's give the second wire guide a try."

We got back to it, and I managed to stay alert through the rest of the procedure. It took an hour and a half before both wires were in place and I was wheeled to surgery. As we entered the surgical suite, I was relieved. I knew I'd be asleep for what came next. Before I lost Shaun, I'd always harbored a fear of dying under general anesthesia, but now I hoped I wouldn't have to wake up again. I thought how I could be minutes away from seeing Shaun, and the prospect gave me a sense of peace. It may sound heartless, but I wanted a reprieve from the unrelenting grief I was living with.

Clearly, God had other plans for me. I woke in recovery to learn that the tumor which we thought was the size of a marble was closer to the size of an egg. The doctor had enlarged the area of removal, but he wasn't certain that he'd gotten it all out. When the report came back, he saw that the margins were narrow, which meant there could be traces of cancerous tissue left in my breast. I had some important decisions to make.

After several appointments with different doctors, talking with other breast cancer survivors, and reading endless articles, I decided to check breast cancer off my list for good. I didn't have room in my brain to entertain grief and breast cancer at the same time. Since I couldn't conveniently rid myself of my grief, I elected to do what would allow me to put cancer out of my mind once and for all—I chose to have a double mastectomy. I figured since they were already watching a spot on the other breast, I might as well be done with both. I wanted to put cancer behind me as fast as possible, not play a waiting game. This was the best way to achieve that.

The mastectomy surgery went as planned, and I woke knowing I was cancer-free. This was a great relief, but I didn't bounce back very quickly. For months, I questioned if what I had done was right. My chest was scarred, and reconstruction surgery was going to take time. I berated myself, wondering why, for once in my life, hadn't I taken the easy route? I'd had the option of taking a more conservative route and letting them remove more tissue from the right breast and keep an eye on the left one for six months—why hadn't I tried that first? I had always had a tendency to deal with things with an all-or-nothing mindset, and I'd handled this the same way. Now, I regretted it. With my breasts removed, I felt I'd lost another part of my identity, a part that was also related to motherhood.

I couldn't look in the mirror for weeks. When I finally did, it was as startling as I expected. The reconstruction process was ahead of me, and it would turn out to be much more difficult and time-consuming than I was first led to believe. It didn't go smoothly and required several revisions through multiple surgeries. Every time I went under anesthesia, my thoughts were on Shaun. I prayed that if I didn't make it, God would allow us to be together again. After the process was complete, I felt better about myself. But when my friends and colleagues looked at me, I wondered if they'd forever see somebody who had lost not only her child, but her breasts as well.

People asked me if the surgery was difficult to endure. I will tell you that compared to losing a child, not at all. My incisions healed and scars faded, but my broken heart is forever changed. Today, I consider what I went through to be part of my accumulated battle scars of life. Sometimes I think God sent the experience to provide me with a distraction from the heartache I was going through. It forced me to focus on other things and made me attend to my health. I realized how much I was loved and needed by my family, and most of all, it showed me that God wanted me to live. I began to believe that a pathway to recovery existed somewhere, and I could feel my heart begin to soften a little, warmed by a flicker of hope.

Journal Entry
October 1, 2009
Dear Shaun,

Today, I was diagnosed with breast cancer. In my heart, I know it was because I lost you. I think I wanted to die so God gave me this battle to fight. Maybe he wants to show me that I want to live.

Love and miss you,
Mom

CHAPTER THIRTEEN

SIGNS FROM SHAUN

I felt you in the breeze today, it was like a whisper from Heaven.
—*Cindy Baumann*

IT WAS EXTREMELY hard for me to go from daily conversations with Shaun to nothing. As a mother, my focus was on his protection and care. I was left with so many unanswered questions. It's impossible to turn off the mother switch overnight. I needed to know he was safe.

In my attempt to connect with Shaun, I read books on every topic imaginable and reached out to priests, ministers, counselors, spiritual healers, and mediums. Most people I've talked to are open to the idea of asking for help from the first three, but not the last two. They sometimes feel that spiritual healers don't work, and mediums are either fake or talking to the devil or that it's all "woo-woo."

I believe when a loved one dies, their spirit stays close for a while, maybe for the purpose of helping us cope. The transition is a huge adjustment for everyone, and it takes time. I had a number of experiences that proved to me this is true, and many people have shared with me their own moments of connection with loved ones who have passed as well. Shaun sent me all kinds of signs, both religious and non-traditional. It just took me a while to believe that what I was experiencing was real.

One of the most undeniable signs from Shaun occurred not long after he died. In my bedroom, I had glass angels that could be turned on and off with a switch on the bottom. At random times during the day, one of them would light up. At first, I thought the kids were turning them on so I would think it was Shaun and feel comforted, but one night as I was crying, one of the angels lit up by itself. As the intensity of my crying increased, the angel shone brighter until the room was covered in a heavenly blue light. I knew it was Shaun reaching out to me.

Another sign that caught my attention was the right song playing on the radio at a coincidental moment with a meaningful message in the lyrics, such as "Angel" by Sarah McLachlan and "Forever Young" by Rod Stewart. The repeating of certain numbers, such as 11:11 or 1:11 on my phone or car clock was another. I'd see them and instantly have a feeling Shaun was nearby. I'd never heard of the phrase "pennies from heaven" until I lost Shaun, and then they showed up in the most unusual places. I would find a single penny in the bottom of my dresser drawer, or underneath the mat in my car. Many times, as I got out of my car, there was a shiny copper penny. Funny how it was right outside my car door in a huge parking lot. Of course, I always picked them up and thanked Shaun for the message.

There is no shortage of reports from people who experience dream visitations from deceased loved ones. These reports vary from a brief scene where the loved one lets their family member know they are well to detailed encounters that deliver specific information, such as where they hid the important documents everybody's been searching for.

To my great joy, I also saw Shaun in my dreams. Some of my dreams of him were comforting, but others were not. For example, at times I dreamed Shaun was alive and the entire world was hiding him from me. It was like he was part of a big conspiracy, and they had to protect him. In these dreams, he seemed weak and frail, as though he was struggling to recover from the gunshot wound. Of course, this was not true; from what I've learned, the disturbing dreams were the product of anxiety and fear.

At other times, my dreams felt like a true visitation. I could hear Shaun's voice and feel him embracing me. In those moments, I would hold him as tightly as I could; I never wanted to let him go. The love I felt in those dreams was unbelievable. During one of the most intense dreams, we were sitting facing each other and he had a hand on each of my shoulders. I could feel his hands on me, strong and warm. He was wearing his wedding tux, and as he stared into my tear-filled eyes, I felt the compassion pouring out of his heart.

He said, "I know this has been hard on you, Mom. I'm sorry, but it was meant to be. There was nothing anybody could have done. I am happy here, and I'm still with you. We will be together again, I promise."

"But when?"

"I don't know when you are slated to come."

I knew this was something Shaun had learned from God because he would never have used those particular words. Such dreams brought me a sense of peace and wonder, and I always longed for the next.

I prayed that Fran would also have a sense of Shaun's presence. He had suffered so much, and I wanted something to bring him comfort. Losing Shaun was by far the lowest point in his life. He felt life had cheated both him and his son. After Shaun died, Fran didn't like weddings, birthdays, or celebrations, and even had a hard time when his nephews or nieces had children. This was because he longed to be celebrating Shaun's children. He prayed to God for an understanding of how he could allow it to happen.

One day, about four months after the accident, he was driving to work and found himself seventy miles away from his destination, kneeling on the ground where Shaun had been shot. He was crying when suddenly he felt God wrap his arms around him, saying, "I am always here."

Fran told me about another experience that was profoundly meaningful to him and helped him to turn the corner in his grief. One Father's Day he was praying to God before he went to sleep, asking if Shaun was okay. Fran always dreams in black and white, but that night he saw Shaun in vivid color. He was dressed in a soft white robe that embraced his body and had a sparkling diamond stud in his ear, something he had wanted to wear when he was alive but was afraid he'd be teased about.

Shaun's entire being glowed with an array of beautiful, brilliant colors unlike anything Fran had ever seen on Earth, and they were shining right through him. All Fran had to do was think of a question, and Shaun would answer him without speaking. At the end of the dream, he said, "Dad, I'll always be with you." This dream gave Fran a tremendous sense of peace and comfort, and although it took many more years of healing, Fran feels he is right with God again. He misses Shaun, but on those tough days, he sees the light a little sooner. Today, when Shaun's birthday rolls around, it is a celebration for Fran, a day of gratitude for the beautiful gift he was to us.

My mother was blessed with an angelic visit of Shaun as well. In her dream, they were seated together in the balcony of a church. Mom was so surprised to see him that she reached out to touch his face to see if he was really there. His skin was unbelievably pure and delicate, and she said to him, "Shaun, your skin is so soft." He looked at her and smiled. They spent a little time together, and when Mom sensed it was time to say goodbye, she leaned over to kiss him on the cheek. Shaun smiled and said, "Please give my mom a kiss from me." Seeing Shaun so healthy and happy was so real to my mother, it left her with a feeling of deep and abiding joy.

The experiences of other people who have encountered their departed loved ones have been inspirational to me too. A good friend told me the night her father died, she saw him in her dream. He was asleep, snoring as usual, and she shook him awake, excited and amazed to see he was alive. He sat up and told her to let him rest because he was exhausted, but urged her to tell her boss to fix the roof of one of the buildings used by the agency she worked for, or it was going to cave in and hurt somebody. She didn't go to work the next day, but received a call at home from a work colleague telling her that the owner of the building had discovered the roof was dangerous and had evacuated everybody until the situation could be assessed. The maintenance of the building was not something my friend was involved with at work, so she knew nothing about the roof problem beforehand. This was confirmation for her that she had communicated with her father in her dream the night before.

My son Justin also had an incredible encounter. One day, when he was about ten years old, he nonchalantly told me, "Mom, Jesus came to visit me today."

"Really? Did you invite him in?"

"Yes, but he didn't want to come in, so we sat out on the granite bench in front of the house and talked."

I replied, "What did you talk about?"

"Just stuff. Then he had to leave."

"Wow, that's pretty cool he came to visit us."

He answered simply, "Yes."

Justin had never had imaginary friends, but he would sometimes wake up and say he had people in his room at night. I told him not to be afraid as they were angels, and to talk to them. He said he just wanted me to know and that it didn't frighten him. From the age of two years old, he would wake up from a nap saying the name *Jesus*. We had a Christian home and believed in God, but we didn't practice our prayers as much as we should. This little boy was meeting God in his dreams and continued to be visited throughout his years at home. His extra dose of faith gave us strength after we lost Shaun.

Shaun tried to communicate with us in many other ways. Before the digital age, we sent a lot of films out to be developed. Sometimes we held onto the rolls for a long time after the pictures were taken but before processing, so it could be a surprise to find out what was on them when they came in the mail. There were occasions when a random orb appeared in the photographs. For those who aren't familiar with orbs, they are circles of light that appear without any explainable reason in photographs, and they are understood to be the presence of a spirit. We had many such photographs. There were pictures of the kids with orbs near them, and Christmas photos of the family opening gifts where a single orb appeared—just one, for the person missing in our family.

My parents also had orbs appear in their photographs. On a trip to Horsetail Falls in Mexico, they took a digital picture, and it was filled with orbs. They certainly had a lot of loved ones with them on that trip; both of their parents, a brother, sister, nephew, aunts, uncles, cousins, and of course Shaun. When my mother told me about this incident, she also shared a story about the church in the small town I grew up in. Over the years, it had deteriorated, and the membership built a new one. A gentleman bought the old church and was removing the light fixtures, stained-glass windows, and artifacts from the church. To catalog the removal, he was taking pictures along the way for his records; to his surprise, they were filled with orbs.

A friend of mine had enormous orbs show up in her photographs as well, each one about four feet across. While she was taking the pictures, she noticed they only were visible on statues of angels. As an experiment, she said aloud, "If this is you, Mom, I need to see *two* orbs, one over each of the chairs in the garden." She took another picture, and two large orbs were there, directly above the chairs.

Another sign for me took the form of birdsong. When I went to work, it seemed that mourning doves followed me. They sat outside my window on the telephone wire and cooed. They were so loud that I could hear them through the building and glass windows. It seemed they caught my attention when I needed it most. No matter where we went, they appeared in the trees around us. I considered them messengers from heaven and was so thankful that they followed me.

I did some research to see if there was any spiritual symbolism with the mourning dove, and what I discovered gave me another confirmation that God was seeking to comfort me through these lovely creatures. I learned they symbolize three beautiful principles: the Holy Spirit, hope, and peace, and that beyond their sorrowful song is a message of life, hope, and renewal. Butterflies carried a similar message, as they landed on me and stayed with me for a few seconds. There was a particular kind of bright blue iridescent butterfly that seemed to hang around when I sat on the step near the pond by my house. It would fly away and then circle back as if it was reassuring me that Shaun was nearby, and his soul was safe.

It became obvious that I wasn't going to get a magical physical appearance where my son would stop by for a visit, appear to me, and calm my soul. Desperate for some sort of two-way communication, I visited some mediums. While my experiences were positive, I have heard of others that have negative stories to tell. I understand the reasons why some people are wary of mediums and others are comfortable with them. Throughout the Bible, trying to communicate with the dead is discouraged (see Leviticus 19:31). Yet, there are also many scriptural accounts where people received information about the future, or messages from their departed loved ones through visitation, dreams, and advisors (see 1 Samuel 28). Being a Christian with a strong belief in God, I had mixed feelings, but I was desperate to hear from my son and would have tried anything to communicate with him. At the time, this helped me feel closer to Shaun.

First, I visited a medium named Darlene who is often sought out by many Christians. She is an ordained minister, and my experience with her was very positive. Darlene validated things that only Shaun knew. She referenced an issue with Shaun's teeth that was going on just before he died. He'd had a temporary filling in November but waited until January when his insurance would start over to complete the treatment. I'd encouraged him to wait, but now I wish I had paid for it, so he could've finished it. Darlene also tuned into the meniscus surgery performed on Kevin's knee. She was able to sense who was supportive of me and who couldn't be supportive. She identified loved ones who were with Shaun in the afterlife, including my grandma; a first cousin, Kyle; a grandpa; and a neighbor, Terry, who died in a drowning accident decades ago. Darlene said that Shaun was around us often and assured me that all of our love reached him.

Through her, Shaun said, "Mom, you mean the world to me."

She brought up the story of the haircut I gave Shaun and how much we'd laughed about it. She talked about a birthday coming up and how much he wanted us to celebrate it, and said Shaun was acknowledging the scholarship we set up in his memory. Darlene referred to Shaun as an old soul and saw that we had an unbelievable connection. She said it was something she'd never seen before. She told me Shaun carried positive energy within his soul, and was confident in his journey, both in life and death. She assured me that his transition was easy and smooth—he walked through a doorway into a beautiful light. I remembered the portal of light I had seen on my way to the hospital the night he'd died and was sure I'd witnessed it opening up to receive him.

Shaun said, "I knew where I was going, and I am okay."

Darlene said Shaun told her about an auto accident Kevin and the boys were in. She knew details, such as who was driving, and the fact that Justin was sleeping and woke up as they rolled down the road. These were things she could know only if Shaun was there to see them. It was clear to me that my son helped protect his friends and brothers that day.

As the reading continued, she identified our cabin up north with a reference to slalom skiing. She said Shaun was encouraging me to get back out there and enjoy the sport we had shared. This made me aware that when we participate in things our loved ones enjoyed, they are able to connect with us more closely. Darlene commented on how particular Shaun was with his clothing and appearance. The mention of a black onyx ring he gave to Julia came up, and he told us that Julia would be dancing soon with a boy and girl around her, signifying two possible children. She also mentioned the pennies and the numbers 1:11 as a sign of his presence.

One of the main points Shaun made through Darlene was to remember the joy. He reminded me that everybody, especially the boys, watched me to see how I was coping. He said they were concerned about me, and it was an added strain on them. They needed reassurance that I was all right. He urged me to take part in more creative outlets, saying he saw me with a paintbrush. I had never painted before, but he was right—it was a hobby I would take up. He also encouraged me to acclimate to the changes in my life and be open about where they were leading me. He even mentioned that I would work with people and help them with grief—something I'm currently involved with. He said he wanted me to read the Bible and listen to my inner voice. He said, "All will be well," and told me that I should help others through their grief.

The readings helped me to understand that my son is still my son, and he cares about me. I knew Shaun was telling me, "Find peace, Mom. It is all about love and forgiveness."

In one of the sessions, Shaun mentioned that he was worried about his older brother, so I invited Ryan to come along to a session, thinking it might help him heal. Shaun mentioned the knife that was in Ryan's pocket, something only Shaun would have known. He then referenced the hunting accident and Ryan's response to it.

"When Ryan realized I had been shot by another hunter, he picked me up. Tears were running down his face. He went to move something and doubted his strength, but his superpower kicked in and he did it."

He said, "If it was reversed, Ry, and you were on this side, you wouldn't want me beating myself up about the accident. You were supposed to be there that day. You had a part, and you did everything right. You did everything you could at the scene—it was just my time to go."

The fact that Shaun used his brother's nickname, Ry, was significant—only Maria and Shaun called him Ry.

Shaun told Ryan to remember the good times. "Please look at moments of fun, not death. Remember when we laughed about the cake? You were so funny." He also addressed the anger in Ryan. "This doesn't make sense now, but it will get better with time." He asked Ryan to forgive the person who shot him. "It will take time, but please forgive him. It was an accident." He stressed that Ryan should not stop living because his brother is not here to walk through life beside him. "Think about the things I would have done if I had lived. Have your purpose in life and live it."

Shaun told Ryan that he was very much alive, and he knew Ryan would have children to love one day. He referred to their biological father, Fran, and said he thinks of him every day and can feel the prayers his father says for him. Shaun said he is aware that Fran lives with regrets about many things and acknowledged that his father had turned his life around and was a good role model. These statements were very accurate and helped us in the process of healing.

Sometime later, I had another remarkable experience with a very famous medium. I'd been scouring his website and reading his books, which provided me with much comfort. His was the first book I read that gave me hope. He talked about how beautiful life in heaven is, and how much guidance and peace our loved ones receive there. He described how they are connected to us spiritually and how they remain aware of what is happening in our lives.

In 2011, before the fourth anniversary of Shaun's death, I reached out to him on one of his Facebook posts. This is my message to him: *I lost my son on 11-24-07. It will be four years on Thanksgiving Day. What a tough holiday. The journey has been difficult, and I miss him every minute of every day. He was my best friend. I wonder if he is lonely? Does he have friends? What does he do all day? Does he miss me? And does he see how much his brothers miss him? I love and miss him so much.*

After I posted it, I watched for a response. I understand he has thousands of followers, a number that grows daily, so how could he possibly respond to my post? You can imagine my surprise when on November 29, there was this message from him:

Cindy, I hope you will appreciate this story. We went through all the posts today to try and answer them all, but after my sessions this morning, a young man in spirit hung around and kept saying, 'You missed one.' I ignored it, but spirit came back and repeatedly said, 'You missed a post.' So, I asked my assistant to check the posts and lo and behold, we had missed yours. He kindly helped me get back onto the site via phone (it's now 11:30 pm) to let you know that your son cares so much about you and the family that he insisted I send you a post tonight, without fail. I hope it helps you understand how much you are loved and cared for, and how much the souls are thinking of our best interests and emotional well-being. The souls live in a world of love and joy, and part of their joy is to help us understand it is only a matter of time before we see them again in a beautiful world. And please remember to thank your son for being so persistent and making an old man stay up past his bedtime to make sure your post was answered.

That message brought hope and a smile to my face. I had peace that night, and I hope to visit him in person someday.

My journey without Shaun was a winding road with many twists, turns, and dead ends, but without fail, God spoke to me in a million different ways, meeting me wherever I was to let me know I was not alone in my sorrow. He is real and He has allowed Shaun to express his love to me in many forms, including through dreams, symbols, signs, and people gifted with a high degree of intuition. Every time some form of spiritual communication has occurred, my heart has been soothed and strengthened, and I've grown more certain of God's love and Shaun's well-being. I have no doubt that our loved ones visit us often, and at rare and precious times, their light can be seen. I will always hold Shaun's visits and signs in safekeeping in my heart.

Journal Entry
December 22, 2007
Dear Shaun,

I saw Darlene today. You communicated to her that as a child, you had all you ever wanted, and you were happy. You said I was a good mom, and I did my best to protect you. About the accident . . . you said, "There was nothing you could have done. It's like I knew I was in grave danger. I knew I wouldn't make it. God and Mary were there to take me. I didn't suffer at all. There were a lot of shots, the man didn't mean it. Mom, I heard you scream. You were the first one to know I was gone. It was so painful because I had to pass through your heart."

Darlene saw you at the wedding, you were happy and dancing. She knew you were sensitive and gentle. She said I raised you to be a good man. You snagged Julia because of this and gave yourself to her. Darlene was great! She said you mentioned that Ryan did his best and you wanted me to keep an eye on him.

You commented, "I don't know why I was called home other than I can help more people from here. I have my wings and they work."

Shaun, I sure hope that was you who communicated with us because everything I heard made me feel good, other than not being able to hold you. Please guide me.

I love you so much,
Mom

CHAPTER FOURTEEN

THE EMPTY NEST

Missing you comes in waves, and tonight I'm drowning.
—*Chris Young*

TWO YEARS AFTER Shaun died, Jordan graduated from high school. His school had a long-standing tradition where seniors wrote a letter to their parents, and the parents wrote to their kids. Our letter to Jordan expressed that we understood how tough high school was for him after Shaun died and how proud we were of his achievement, while Jordan's letter to us was an apology. He explained how he was full of anger and hadn't known what to do with it, so he released it on those who were closest to him. I knew that Jordan had weathered much of his grief alone, as the rest of us were so immersed in our sadness to be of much comfort. Knowing this brought me to tears. I wished I'd been more available to him, but I wasn't capable at the time. Jordan understood, because he was in the same broken state, but still, as a mother, it hurt deeply to think how alone he had felt during his last two years of high school.

His letter also said he hoped that one day he'd do something with his life that Shaun would be proud of. This was no surprise, since Shaun had been much more than a big brother to Jordan—he was his close friend and a role model in every way.

The plan had always been that after graduation Jordan and Justin would move to Madison where Shaun went to college. For years, they'd talked about the fun they'd have once they were away from home and living in the same town. They loved each other so much and wanted to stay close during adulthood, but they'd been forced to let go of that dream. Now, Jordan wasn't ready to leave home after graduation. He wanted to stay close to his family so his heart could continue healing, and we really wanted the extra time with him. He chose to attend the local college, while Justin completed his last two years of high school. He would wait for his younger brother, and they would go to Madison together.

Justin's last two years of high school went by quickly, and before I knew it, he was graduating too. I realized that time had gone by in a blur, and as I took stock, I saw how much I'd missed during my sons' high school years. I had been there physically but not emotionally. I'd attended the prom and high school grand march appearances, but I was absent for many of the school functions and sporting events. I had been too broken to be their mother. Grief, followed by breast cancer and even more years of grief, had taken those special times away from us, and there was no way to recover them.

I don't think Justin's classmates comprehended how difficult those years were for him. Like his brothers, he had to work through his emotions alone, but his faith was deep, and it helped us keep our faith alive. I never doubted that God was present in Justin's life. Still, I had to dig deep and call on St. Francis's words in the Serenity Prayer: "Help me to change the things I can, to accept the things I cannot change, and to have the wisdom to know the difference."

Shaking off my regrets, I looked for how I could step up to the plate in the present. The school needed help with the food committee for the senior party, so I signed up, hoping to be of use again. I also wanted to see the other parents to apologize for my absence in the last few years and personally thank those who had supported Justin when I couldn't. Once the meeting was underway, however, I couldn't bring myself to speak up. I was afraid if I talked about how I felt, the emotions would kick in and I'd make everybody uncomfortable. The old feeling of panic came over me, and I struggled to breathe, which forced me to sit in silence. After the meeting was over, I reached out to some of the parents through private email to express my heartfelt thanks to them. I hope if other parents from the school read this book, they will understand the depth of my gratitude for their kindness and help through those years, especially for those who supported my son on the golf team.

As we went through the letter-writing tradition with Justin, I searched for words that would capture how much I loved and understood him. Our letters to him expressed the depth of our love, grief, and faith, and Justin's made it clear how much Shaun had impacted his life. Shaun had always been right there to help or teach his brother or anyone else who needed him. He was never selfish with his time. Justin also expressed how his faith pulled him through.

When graduation day came, I knew it would be difficult for everyone. Like our other family celebrations, the day was filled with mixed emotions. We knew we had much to be grateful for, yet the sense that Shaun was missing was always with us—the emptiness could be felt through the whole house. Still, my heart soared with pride as I watched Justin accept his diploma. I knew that, just like Jordan, he had a bright future.

After graduation, the plans we'd had for the boys' college education were set in motion. Even though their original reason for choosing Madison was gone, Justin and Jordan were excited to launch themselves into the next phase of their lives. When it was time for the boys to pack up and go, it was bittersweet. As we moved them into their apartment, I noticed all the pictures they'd brought along included Shaun. There were photos of the four boys when they were young, Shaun's wedding picture, and the first time Shaun took Justin bowhunting. It was touching to see how they'd found a way to take Shaun to Madison with them after all. I was proud of their courage to follow through with their plans despite what they'd been through, and I knew Shaun was proud of them too.

Kevin and I were now empty nesters, which brought new emotional challenges. Our house went from being action-packed to eerily silent, adding to the emptiness we felt. Memories continued to flood my mind, and I was haunted with thoughts about the life Shaun had left unfinished. In my mind's eye, I could see what might have been. I imagined him taking his children on a walk in the woods, reading to them, and teaching them to ski. I bet his bright smile would have deepened the little creases around his eyes, making him even more attractive.

He and Julia would have been busy building the life they'd dreamed of. Sometimes I would open an album and look at photos of when Shaun was a little boy and wish I could smile, or maybe even laugh. But instead, I'd worry that I was going to forget something he did as a child . . . the funny things he said, his school-year antics, whether it was the right arm or the left arm that he broke, or the millions of other details that make up a child's precious little life.

After Justin and Jordan moved out, Kevin and I decided to face cleaning Shaun's room. I'd found it impossible to discard anything that belonged to him and had kept everything just like he'd left it. The last clothes he wore before going hunting that day were draped over the edge of his bed, waiting for him to come home and put them on. His belt hung through half of the belt loops of his pants, and the top of his cologne lay beside the bottle. It was time to put things away.

Kevin helped me pick up a few things and threw away a half-full bottle of Gatorade. I wanted to open it and press my lips on it, but Kevin stopped me. It was hard throwing something away that he had touched. His impression lived on it. Deodorant, toothpaste, his toothbrush—I didn't know what to do with these personal items. He was in that room, and I didn't want to let him go. This might sound crazy to some people, but it's all I had left.

Several months later, my mom asked if she could come to wash his bedding while I was at work. The only thing I needed to do was pick up the comforter from the dry cleaners. And, if that was too hard, she would come back and pick it up. It was a hard day knowing another piece of him was being washed away. I was grateful that my mom was there to do it. I still have some of his clothing sealed in Ziploc bags. It's my way of saving his scent.

It was a significant turning point for us to face cleaning the room. I understand that everyone's grief journey is unique, and some people need to distance themselves from their loved one's belongings, while others want to spend time near them. I chose to sleep with one of Shaun's shirts under my pillow. A friend of mine kept a gold scarf across the floor where the hospice bed had been in her house, because her mother died in that spot, and to her, it was a sacred location. She didn't want people walking over it with their dirty shoes. After five years, she was ready to move the scarf, but she still walked around the edge of the room as if the bed was there. Finally, she rearranged the furniture so the area wouldn't be stepped on. Her sister, on the other hand, didn't step foot in the house for ten years after her mother died. Both honored what they needed to do, and neither judged the other for it.

These dark years were brightened by a lovely ray of sunshine on June

11, 2011. On that day, my granddaughter Braelynn Belle was born, and my heart burst with joy for the first time in years. We were excited and happy to have our first girl in the family. She's a beautiful little gift from God, and her arrival signaled the start of more healing. She's surrounded by doting uncles, grandparents, and great-grandparents. I'm so grateful she is in my life; it's a joy and honor to watch her grow. Of course, I wish Shaun was here to be with Braelynn. He would have been an awesome uncle to her. He loved kids and had more patience than all of us put together.

When she was about five years old, I said something about Shaun, and Braelynn said brightly, "I know Uncle Shaun. He's my best friend."

I said, "He's my best friend too, and I miss him so much."

How does she know him? Has he visited her in a dream? Perhaps he sent her off with some words of wisdom and a kiss for luck! I have a feeling that is the case.

Soon, I was back at work and busy as ever, but still struggled with depression and feeling distracted. Before Shaun's death, I had looked forward to meeting new people and building personal relationships, but after he died, my confidence evaporated. I became afraid to interact with potential customers for fear they would ask me, "How many kids do you have?" Saying that I had three sons felt like a lie and a betrayal of Shaun, but if I answered the question honestly, I could see they wished they had never asked.

I wanted to crawl in a corner and hide from the world, but my team and clients needed me. I had to give what I could, even if it was an incomplete me. I was blessed by several team members, clients, and friends who consistently checked in on me. They have no idea how much that meant. There were days when their encouragement literally kept me alive.

My business partner struggled with the new me, and no wonder—I was a different person. The outgoing, capable woman she had gone into business with was gone, replaced by a withdrawn, heavy-hearted person. When people asked how things were going, she would jump in and say I was doing fine, because that was what she wanted to believe, but it was far from the truth. I had many breakdowns at the office, and our partnership became very strained during this time. We had disagreements, and I could see the frustration and fear in her face. She couldn't comprehend the level of absolute devastation I was dealing with.

It was clear to everyone that something had to change. My team felt the tension in the air between my partner and me. It was like when Mommy and Daddy fight—the kids know it, and everybody's confused and uncomfortable. We had to figure out where the business would go from here. I didn't want to lose the company I'd worked hard to create, so I managed to dredge up a new mask to wear so I could "pretend better." That was what they wanted to see, so I faked it until I could make it.

Keeping up with the workload while hurting inside was exhausting, and when the long days ended and I could go home, I felt a tremendous sense of relief. Once there, I could take off the mask and my suit of armor and just be my weak, vulnerable, broken self. I would anesthetize myself with a few drinks or a sleeping pill, try to fall asleep, and hope the next day would be different, but of course it wasn't. It was a short-term fix to help endure the pain.

Life became a blur with little participation on my part. Half the time, I didn't feel like I was in my body. I was detached from everything except grief. It was the only thing left that felt real. At least my broken heart was something I could bond with. Looking back, I think that in a strange way I thought if I couldn't connect with Shaun in life, at least I could stay connected to him through pain.

My thoughts ran the gamut from "Who am I?" to "Is this a parallel life, and my son is still alive somewhere, but I just can't see him?" One moment, I'd feel like I was a spectator watching a movie trailer without sound, and in the next moment it would dawn on me that it was my own life I was watching. Sometimes I thought I was going crazy, and I wished that were the case. If I were really insane, maybe it wouldn't keep hurting so much.

As much as I wanted to be free, I couldn't find the tools I needed to chisel my way out of my prison. This was the cycle I was trapped in for longer than I believed was possible. I began to see that my grief over Shaun was like a fog. I couldn't see any beauty in my life because my vision was blocked by thick clouds. Yes, there had been glimmers of light through the years, and I'd made some progress, but always found myself back at the edge of that whirlpool of sadness. I was afloat in my rowboat without any direction. I had to find a better way.

Not one to give up, I began to search again for something that would give me an edge up. All the books I read underscored the importance of gratitude, so I started incorporating this attribute into my nightly prayers. At first, it seemed impossible, but I got in the habit of counting my blessings, even when I didn't feel like it. Over time, I could tell my mind was defaulting more and more often to thoughts of thankfulness rather than ruminating endlessly over the tragedies of my life. In essence, I was re-training my brain.

This practice dissipated some of the clouds that surrounded me and allowed me to glimpse the light illuminating the edge of the fog. As I drew closer to that light, I saw more beauty waiting for me beyond it, and it gave me the courage I needed to keep rowing toward that distant shore of peace. Here's one of my gratitude lists:

I can see, hear, walk, and speak.
I have a home and a warm bed.
I have food on my table.
I'm part of a loving family.
I have children, a granddaughter, and a husband to love.
I share a deep and eternal love with Shaun.
I have opportunities to uplift others.
I have loyal grief dogs who never leave my side.
I can feel the warm sunshine on my face.
We live in a beautiful world, full of kind, caring people.
I had the incredible gift of being Shaun's mom.
Shaun continues to bring joy to my life.
Most of all—I know the God of the Universe is taking care of my son.

I encourage you to take time to make a list of the blessings that surround you. Even if you feel you are just going through the motions as you do it, if you persevere, it may prove to be the key to relief you are seeking. The following words helped me: "Practicing gratitude doesn't mean suppressing painful feelings or ignoring the pain in the world. It means seeing the good that exists along with the bad."

Journal Entry
June 8, 2009

Jordan graduated from high school, and we sure missed you. He wrote a very special letter to us and talked about how hard it has been since we lost you. He misses you a lot. You already know that. We lost so much when we lost you.

We had a graduation party, and I felt a void all day. You should have been here with us. Julia and her parents came over. It is still so hard seeing her without you. You were soul mates and I loved seeing you together. You loved each other so much. Were you here with us? I don't feel you around, Shaun. I wish I could see you in the flesh one more time and hug you goodbye. I want to see the love and happiness on your face, and I want peace in my heart. This is a hard life. Losing you zapped me of my passions. It's hard to get up and face the world every day. Please take care of Jordan as he gains independence. I want him to fulfill his dreams, but I'm scared. Please watch over all the kids, and Kevin. I can't lose another; my heart can't take it. I don't think there's anything worse than a shattered heart.

I pray for your presence. I will love you forever,
Mom

Journal Entry
January 17, 2011
Dear Shaun,

Well, today we went in for Ryan and Maria's ultrasound. It was so neat seeing the baby's hands, arm, and face. We got a great foot shot. Yes, she's going to have Maria's feet. The second toe looks much longer than the big toe. And we found out it's a girl. What a nice surprise. We would have been happy with a boy, but I must say it's going to be fun having a little girl around. I think Ryan and Maria were pleased as well. Now, it's pink all the way. Sure wish you were here.

Love you,
Mom

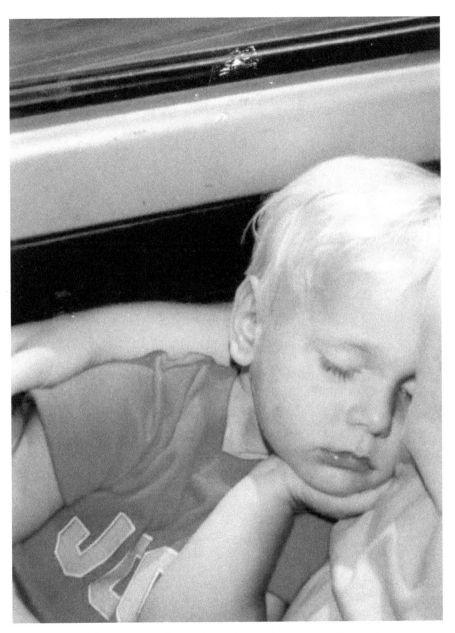

1983, Shaun age 2, after a chemotherapy treatment. So precious.

1995, (L to R) Shaun, Jordan, Ryan and Justin. Brotherly love.

1996, (L to R) Kevin, Jordan, Shaun, me, Ryan and Justin. Happiness!

2002, (L to R) Shaun, Kevin and Jordan. Canada fishing trip.

2006, Julia and Shaun. Enjoying the sunset.

2006, Shaun and his father, Fran. Canada fishing trip.

2007, Julia and Shaun on their wedding day. Pure love!

2007, Shaun and I on his wedding day. A day of love and profound joy.

2013, me and my parents at Christmas. Shaun joined us in spirit (orb on the left).

2016, (L to R) Kevin, me, Justin, Maria, Braelynn, Ryan and Jordan. Furry family (Lexi and Sami). Christmas at the cabin.

2018, (L to R) Justin, Jordan, me, Kevin, Braelynn, Maria and Ryan.
Beneath Shaun's memorial magnolia tree.

2018, (L to R) Kevin, me and Fran. After releasing Shaun's ashes.

2019, (L to R) Jordan, Ryan, Braelynn and Justin. Grateful for each other.

CHAPTER FIFTEEN

THE DEPTH OF MY PAIN

The bravest thing I ever did was continuing my life when I wanted to die.
—Juliette Lewis

SOME YEARS AFTER the loss of Shaun, I watched as my family members moved on, doing the things they enjoyed. I wanted this for them, of course, but it was in stark contrast to what I was experiencing. Their ability to enjoy life magnified my pain; I wondered if I would ever be able to do the same. The ten-day annual fishing trip rolled around again, and Kevin, Jordan, and Justin made their plans to leave. I knew I would be worried sick, counting the days until they returned home safely. It hurt to think that Shaun was missing the event again, and I couldn't bear the thought of being home alone for such a long time. I hated it.

A few days after they left, I looked out my kitchen window at the lovely day before me. The sun was shining, and the water glistened as if it was covered in diamonds, but in my heart, there was so much darkness. I went onto the deck to feel the warmth of the rays on my face and felt a familiar yearning wash over me—the wish that I could go back to the life I had before the loss—to when we were a complete family, full of joy. I missed that so much. The emptiness engulfed me.

I'd worked so hard to process life without Shaun, but it appeared I'd reached a plateau. After years of counseling, I continued to struggle with PTSD and increased anxiety. Despite the improvement I made in some areas, grief still welled up at the most unexpected times. I was trapped in an exhausting loop of one step forward, one step back. It seemed that I would never be free of it.

I could tell this was going to be another one of those days spent in the shadowland of despair, and I desperately wanted to stop what I knew was coming—the waves of sorrow, reliving the sight of Shaun's lifeless body, the tears, fear, and panic, and the torment of unanswered questions and regrets.

For me, the world had become a threatening place where at any moment the most dreadful tragedies could strike. I lived my life frozen by the fear of danger. At times, I was afraid to get in my car and leave the house. People called me Safety Cindy, and I deserved it. Every time I heard an ambulance, I saw my son's body awaiting autopsy. When a fire truck went by, I wondered if it was my house that was burning down. Sad stories on the news broke my heart, and I grieved for the people involved as if I knew them personally. Intrusive flashbacks and emotional outbursts to triggers relating to the day Shaun died kept my adrenal glands on high alert and left me exhausted. There were days when the anxiety was so bad, I thought I was going crazy, but I didn't know how to get off the hamster wheel in my head.

Everybody around me was affected by my irrational fears and chronic worrying. I knew I was driving my husband and kids nuts and believed I was doing more harm than good in their lives. Worst of all, I was certain that I was beyond repair. As I stood on the deck in the warm sunlight that day, I thought about these things and decided there was only one thing I could do to make it all stop: I had to end my life.

"God, I'm done," I said firmly, startling the birds in the garden. "I can't keep living like this. My days are so dark, and I have no passion for life left inside of me. I'm so tired of taking a few steps forward only to fall ten steps back. I'm sad, lonely, and nobody can help me. Grief is so isolating and hopeless. Most importantly, my heart can't take any more."

I went into the kitchen, got out a sharp knife, and rested it across my wrist. The blade felt cool. It was sharp and heavy. I scraped it across my vein as I considered my options. The idea of floating out of my body and far away from this cruel world was irresistible. I imagined Shaun meeting me and helping me cross from this place to the next.

I didn't cut deeply right away. I wondered, *If I cut myself just a little, will the sting distract me from this hurt in my heart?* Then another wave of grief washed over me, and I thought, *Why settle for distracting myself temporarily? I want permanent relief. I should just end it now.*

God was there in an instant, talking me down from the edge of my insanity. I sensed him telling me that my time of death wasn't my choice, and that I had worked way too hard to end my life all alone and in such a tragic way. He said that Shaun was right there with me, and if I could just keep moving forward, I would get to the other shore. But I had no more fight left in me. I believed I was too broken to be of any value in this world. I screamed out, begging him to take me right then and there.

In spite of what I felt to be the voice of God, the compulsion to cut stayed with me and I refused to put the knife down. I disobeyed his command, and with the freedom of choice he allowed me, I kept the knife at my wrist. The faces of my family passed before me—Ryan, Jordan, Justin, Kevin, Braelynn, Maria, my brother, my sisters, and my parents. I knew how selfish it was of me to put them through losing me, but in that moment, I truly believed they'd be better off without the negativity I brought into their lives.

The darkness won—and I cut.

The first one hurt, but I kept cutting. I longed for the pain to be bigger than the grief that was tormenting me, and it helped for a while. Grateful for the reprieve, I did it again. My body numbed to the pain, and I had to cut it several times and go deeper to get the same effect. The blood was pooling on my wrist and dripped onto the floor. I saw Shaun reaching for me and holding me tight. I closed my eyes, wanting to finish it. I wasn't afraid to die, but again I felt God whispering in my ear.

"There is so much more, my child. Don't end it this way. Don't give up. There's peace to be had on the other side of this. You are not alone. And you are needed on this earth."

In that moment, something in me shifted, and I stopped before I cut too deep to turn back. I sat for a long time, staring at my arm, relieved in a way that I had given myself permission to act on the option of suicide and made the choice to stay. I thought about how my loved ones had been through the same loss and had stood by me while struggling with their own pain. A surge of love washed through me, filling me with a new level of determination to be there for them, and I snapped back to reality.

It took a while to stop the bleeding. Once it eased, I bandaged my wrist with trembling hands. Kevin and the boys wouldn't be home for a few days, so there was time to heal. The bracelets and wraps I typically wore around my wrist would be enough to cover it. I was shaken by the experience, but I understood why some people cut themselves in times of despair. For a brief time, it had given me a break from the emotional pain in my heart.

That evening, I reached for the wine bottle, desperate for a sip of hope. I would start out intending to have one drink, but it always ended up being more. The first glass took the edge off and the second made the harshness of life tolerable. I told myself wine was good for my heart, but I knew better. I figured I deserved to have a crutch, considering what I'd endured. I was even tempted to start my day with a shot in my coffee, and I thought about adding cigarettes to my deathly mix—it would speed up the process, and getting sick didn't scare me. Surely dying couldn't be as horrible as what I was going through. I wondered how long I would have to keep living. The idea of waiting for years to be released from my prison was more than I could bear. I didn't want to rely on alcohol to get through the day, but that was my reality. At least I had the willpower to keep the use of alcohol in check—most of the time.

Admitting all of this is terribly hard for me because I love my family so dearly. But I now understand why some people turn to such desperate measures to ease their grief. When someone feels as lost and empty as I did, they reach a point where they think they have nothing worthwhile to offer to anyone.

Nothing mattered, not because the people I loved didn't matter, but because nothing brought me joy anymore. It was like my mind had been taken captive, and as hard as I tried, I couldn't break free enough to experience the happiness available in the present moment. It felt like I was locked in a dark room away from not only Shaun but everything and everyone that I loved. I wanted so much to be myself, to draw close to everyone, but I couldn't find the key to open the door. The last thing I wanted, really, was to die, but I believed I was already emotionally dead, so it seemed to me that it made no difference if my body followed suit. If I couldn't function in this world, I figured maybe I belonged on the "other side."

I was at a dangerous crossroads. I had to get help, or I was going to lose the battle. What I'd tried so far wasn't enough. I reached out to my therapist, and what he suggested I do next, as unusual as it was, would prove to be a turning point. It couldn't have come soon enough.

Journal Entry
November 22, 2011
Dear Shaun,

It seems like forever since I last saw you. These years have been a blur. I'm not sure how I ever survived them. At times I felt like I would never catch my breath or stop crying. I miss you so much. There are a thousand things I miss about you—the way you spent time with us, the times you helped your brothers, and how much you cared for everyone. You were a sensitive son, husband, and brother. And yet, what I miss most is your smile and your cute personality. You could always make me smile; I miss the joy you brought to my life.

Since we lost you, our home is sad. The life and laughter you brought to us are gone. I've been longing for happiness and a sense of peace, but it is so far away.

This year the Worst day of my life falls on Thanksgiving Day. We have decided to stay home and have a non-traditional meal—lasagna. There's a piece for you without mozzarella cheese. I hope you join us. Please send us a sign that you are with us.

What do you think of Braelynn? Isn't she a sweetheart? I sure wish we could watch you together. You were awesome with the kids. I wanted you to have children. What a dream come true that would have been. Please help me on this journey. It's so difficult. Will my marriage survive this? Will we ever be happy again? I call out to you and beg for help. Do you hear me? I don't want to let you down and yet I feel I have so many times. If only I could have half the qualities that you did. Your patience, kindness, compassion, love, and sweetness were a blessing to us all. And I don't think there was a selfish bone in your body. God gave me a wonderful son. He just didn't let me keep you very long.

I ask that you guide your brothers. They need you—all three of them. Ryan misses his best friend. I see the loss in his eyes, and he tries so hard to act strong around me. Thank God for Maria and Braelynn. Maria misses you like a sister. She never takes her heart necklace off.

Jordan and Justin wished you were still in Madison. The three of you would have enjoyed each other. They moved to Madison to follow in your footsteps, Shaun. They were supposed to walk alongside you, not without you. Help them make the right choices, and take care of them. We miss you every minute of every day. And we will love you forever.

Your Mom

CHAPTER SIXTEEN

EMDR

*Courage doesn't always roar. Sometimes courage is the quiet voice
at the end of the day saying, I will try again tomorrow.*
—Mary Anne Radmacher

I HAD USED traditional counseling, spiritual advice, therapeutic hobbies, and the strength of my willpower to cope with my long-term grief. They had brought me far, but not far enough. Now, my therapist, Rick, suggested I try EMDR—eye movement desensitization reprocessing, a technique developed by Francine Shapiro in 1987.

EMDR is a respected method for treating a range of mental health problems, and it's based on the theory that the mind has a mechanism to heal itself of trauma naturally, in the same way that the body has a system for healing. If the shock is too severe, or if it involves long-term abuse, however, the natural ability of the mind to store memories and heal itself becomes damaged. As a result, we shut down, like an overloaded circuit breaker, causing all those disturbing images and raw emotions to become lodged in the limbic system of the brain. Instead of being properly processed and transmuted into an objective, verbal story form, they remain beneath the surface of our emotions and are easily triggered if we see or hear anything that reminds us of the traumatic event. Even if we learn to suppress the memory in part, the anxiety, panic, and anger associated with it can reappear, making our day-to-day existence a struggle. Since I never knew when a memory would be triggered, I carried around a fear of having a panic attack in addition to my fear of the memory itself.

Living with chronic, unrelieved fear is known to cause physical and mental illnesses, both of which I was experiencing. It was encouraging to me when Rick showed me brain scans that had been done before and after EMDR that showed how the therapy integrates thoughts, feelings, and memories in a safe and healthy manner. Rick explained to me that I would be recounting the traumas in my life and watching lights on a bar move from side to side, as well as other methods to stimulate my brain. He warned me that the process would be intense and rapid, and I had to be prepared to feel a wide variety of conflicting and distressing emotions.

Despite my fear of the specific steps that required reliving the most traumatic memories of my life, I agreed to try. It couldn't be any worse than what I was going through on a daily basis. I tackled this next stage with determination, committed to leaving no stone unturned in my quest for healing. The alternative was unthinkable for me and my family.

I remember so clearly the day I arrived at his office for my first session. I entered the building cautiously. I was a mess that day, both emotionally and physically, and prayed I wouldn't run into anybody I knew. When I stepped into the elevator and pushed the button to the third floor, it felt like the walls closed around me. It was all I could do not to press stop, go back to the ground level, and run. My throat started to close, and my heart began to race. Looking for an excuse to back out, I said to myself, What in the world am I doing? I'm not strong enough to go through this. In fact, it will probably make me even worse. But the elevator kept rising . . .

Rick greeted me at his office door. His calm, compassionate manner helped me feel safe. When he asked how I was doing, tears filled my eyes and I answered honestly, "I'm frightened." Rick suggested that rather than jumping to the main event (which we agree is level ten on a scale of one to ten), I should start with something closer to a six or seven. As soon as he said this, I felt some of the tension leave my body. At least for today, I wouldn't have to remove the bandages from the unhealed wound festering in my heart. I thought for a moment before choosing an event that occurred ten years ago—the loss of my home due to a fire for the second time in my life. The first fire, when I was a young, pregnant bride, had taken its toll, but I felt I'd handled it. The second one in 2003, however, had haunted me ever since.

The day of the fire replays in front of me. I can hear the crackle of flames and feel the heat on my face as I watch my beautiful, brand-new house burning down in front of my eyes. The drywall is crumbling onto the polished hardwood floor in the entry. Flames climb the walls to devour the ceiling. I'm standing in the driveway watching the horror unfold, my mind disconnected from my body. My teeth are chattering, and I am shaking all over as if it's freezing cold instead of 75 degrees outside. I don't know what this shaking means, but the EMT standing next to me does—I am going into shock. It's a terrifying sensation, the same one I would experience five years later as I sat next to Shaun's body in the hospital, but that one would be much more intense.

I hear the EMT's voice, but it sounds like it's a million miles away. "We need to take you to the hospital, ma'am. Let us help you."

I reply, "No, please. I can't leave my family. We have to stay together."

In the back of my delusional mind, I think the fire is going to be out soon, the repairs will be minor, and in a few days, we will be sleeping in our beds again. The shaking throughout my body becomes uncontrollable. I squeeze my eyes shut, and my knees buckle. When I open them, I'm on a stretcher, covered with a blanket. They wheel me away from the house, even as I beg them not to. To appease me, they push me down the driveway away from immediate danger, but don't put me in the ambulance. An oxygen mask is placed over my face, but I fight it. It is suffocating me.

"Cindy, just breathe. It will help to calm you," says the EMT, but I'm barely aware of him.

Then I see Shaun leaning over me. His bright blue eyes, so urgent and kind, are staring into mine. "Mom, look at me. Please, look at me," he says. He holds my arms tightly, and I feel such strength and reassurance in his touch. "Stay with us. We need you. You've been through worse than this. You can make it, Mom. I know you can."

After thrashing on the gurney and fighting to get the breathing mask off my face, the oxygen fills my lungs, and I surrender to a wave of dizziness. I feel like I am separating from my body, drifting off to a safer place and time. I can see it clearly: it's a typical Saturday morning with the family. My husband, four sons and I are sitting at the kitchen counter having breakfast in the new home we'd designed together. Every piece of furniture and tiny detail had been selected with care and love, from the décor and contemporary style of cabinet handles to the intricate lighting in every room. It was more than a house—it was our home, and it meant the world to me.

The dream was so real. I could smell the coffee brewing and hear the voices of my boys joking and talking in the background, but too soon, I regain consciousness.

My heart breaks as I realize I was only dreaming. I'm still on the gurney, and the smell of smoke is everywhere. Kevin, Maria, and the boys are clustered around me, looking as dazed as I do. Ice and Kennan lie at our feet. I gather my courage and turn to look back at my home. The flames have stopped, but the house is gutted. We can see straight through the shell. I stare at the arches that had adorned the entryway with such majesty; now they are charred remains. A shiver goes through me. Where are we going to live?

The sound of Justin whimpering jerks me back to reality. "We lost our toys and special blankets, Mom!" he cries. "Everything is burned! All our stuff is gone."

I move into mom mode, fighting the avalanche of emotions about to overtake me. There will be time for tears later. Right now, I have to help my kids through this. "It's okay, Justin," I say, putting on a brave face. "We'll get new ones."

I think how fortunate we are that we'd all managed to get out safely—we had been in different rooms of the house when the fire started. I can't conceive how a small spark in our outdoor fire pit had turned into an inferno within minutes. Later, I learned that a stray ember from the pit was blown into the leaves next to our house. The flames ignited and climbed to the eaves of the second story. Kevin had immediately grabbed a hose, but he couldn't douse the flames fast enough before they rapidly spread everywhere.

We'd called the fire department and got the kids out, grabbing our precious family photo albums as we ran. I didn't want to lose all the beautiful memories of the kids growing up. Neighbors helped us pull out some other belongings before the fire was out of control, and multiple fire trucks arrived from the towns surrounding Wausau. Despite their best efforts, they couldn't save the home we loved. All I could do was stand and watch it burn—just like I'd done when Fran and I lost the farmhouse so long ago. It was the most horrible form of déjù vu I could imagine.

Reliving the events of the fire with my therapist took its toll, and in the middle of describing it, I had a full-blown panic attack. I started trembling, couldn't catch my breath, and my temperature swung from hot to freezing in seconds. I had so many emotions stuffed away inside me that I was bursting at the seams. Life's traumas were piled on top of one another in thick layers of unhealed sorrow. It was more than a human body could handle. My mind descended into chaos and my body followed.

Rick, in his steady, reassuring tone, walked me through the process, giving me the time I needed to get my emotions under control before he took me to the next one. It felt like I had a million slivers of glass in my soul, and we were pulling them out one piece at a time. As agonizing as it was, I knew I had to stay with it to survive. The fire barely scratched the surface of the trauma I was carrying, but it was a start. I'd accumulated so much grief in my life, and it was eating me alive. For the sake of my family, I had to try.

During that session, we explored the aftermath of the fire as well. Shaking from head to toe, I described to him how we navigated that period of time with only the clothes on our backs. Our wonderful friends Roger and Susan graciously took us in, and we all slept in one room together. I could distinctly remember the first shower I took after the fire. The warm water ran down my face and reignited the smell of smoke. In my mind, I could see the flames racing through the house again. I scrubbed my arms so hard that I broke the surface of my skin.

A few days after the fire, we went to a local department store to buy underwear, pajamas, clothes, shoes, school supplies for the kids, and a few things for Kevin and me. Once the boys were in school again, I knew they would improve. Their classmates would be there to help them forget that we had lost our home, at least until they came back after school. Counting on the resiliency of youth, I knew they would bounce back.

I didn't know it at the time, but part of my identity and personal value was wrapped up in my belongings and my home. Without those things, I felt that I was a shadow of myself. It was as if the fire had taken my sense of worth away. I had to occupy my mind with something, so I threw on some clothes and went to the ad agency that I co-owned with my business partner, Chris. The drive to work was surreal, and I pulled into my parking place on autopilot.

Chris headed me off at the door. "Go get some rest, Cindy. After what's happened, you don't need to be here today."

Tears filled my eyes and ran down my cheeks. "Please don't ask me to leave. This is the only thing in my world that hasn't changed. It's my second home. I need to be here."

I had structure at work. I felt safe and knew that I belonged. Every team member in our building was part of my life, and I needed my work family during my crisis more than they needed me. Years of hard work had gone into building the agency, and the reward was a successful company that was respected in the community. I needed everybody to be strong for me, and they didn't let me down. I held myself together long enough to make it to my desk, and I turned to the day's work, grateful for something to focus on other than the horror I had witnessed. It was a long day, but I spent it in a place that represented normal life to me.

When Kevin and I returned to the house to search for anything that had survived, it was a devastating sight. Just like I'd done with Fran after the first house fire, we sifted through the ashes to see what we could salvage. First, we found pieces of clothing, burnt pieces of furniture, and some half-melted toys. Then, to our surprise, we found a plastic rosary and a wooden cross that one of the boys had made in school. Next, we made the astonishing discovery of a paper cross that was only burned along one edge. The crosses came from the upstairs bedrooms, which had been demolished. In the midst of all the destruction, these precious items were intact. The message, "Trust me, I am with you," rang through me, loud and clear.

We bought a camper and put it on our land so that my oldest son, Ryan, and his fiancée, Maria, could live in it and take care of Kennan and Ice. The garage was standing, so we made beds in there for the dogs to give them a sense of familiarity. I went to work, but I wasn't there. My mind kept replaying what had happened. I couldn't shake it. I wanted my beautiful home back. I couldn't bear the thought of going through the steps to recover from our loss. I just wanted to punch the rewind button and make it all go away, and if that couldn't be, I wanted to fast forward my life to a better place.

Rick ended the session by taking me back to a happier place. My mind drifted to a beach in Florida. I could taste the salt and feel the wind in my hair—this was my place of peace. I walked beside the ocean, and I felt the sand crunch beneath my feet. If I kept the sky and the waves in my line of vision, the scars in my heart would have the chance to heal. Turquoise colors filled my mind, and I was able to escape the horrors of the world for a moment.

When I stood up to leave, my legs shook and my head was spinning. I couldn't believe the level of exhaustion I felt. How could I go through another session like that, much less a whole series of them? I couldn't wait to get out of there, and I was sure I'd never return.

CHAPTER SEVENTEEN

OPENING THE FLOODGATES

As I try and recall all of the dreams you had,
mine was wanting to be your mother forever.
—*Cindy Baumann*

RICK UNDERSTOOD MY reluctance to continue EMDR, and through patience and honesty, he helped me find the courage to return to his office and do what needed to be done. In this chapter, I candidly relate some of the thoughts and emotions that flooded through me during the sessions about Shaun. The process was brutal, but I can only reiterate that for me they were invaluable on the road to my healing. We began by revisiting my memory of going to the hospital where they took Shaun's body after he'd been shot. It's one of the worst memories I have of that day, and I really had to dig deep to find the strength to speak about it.

First, I imagined walking down the long, white hallway leading to the room where he was lying. My family was there, lining the walls as I passed. I could see the door to his room. There was so much sadness hovering around the doorway, I didn't want to enter. When I walked into the room, the emotions of helplessness, emptiness, brokenness, and disbelief hit me all at once, racing through me like a wild animal let loose from a pen.

Rick could see my panic rising, and quickly turned on the bar of lights he used whenever the memories were particularly difficult. He directed me to follow the side-to-side movement of the lights with my eyes, but the steady flow of tears made it almost impossible.

The picture in my mind of Shaun lying motionless in the hospital seems totally real. He looks like he's sleeping, as if I could walk over and wake him up. He is a beautiful boy. His hands and feet are perfect. His eyelashes are long, blond, and tipped with black at the ends. Even in death, he looks handsome. When I touch him, he is so cold—so very cold. My fingers start to tingle with a chill. I will never forget that coldness. His life is gone.

As he lays there, I can sense him slipping away from me. He doesn't want to leave. I'm sure he doesn't. He knows it will nearly kill me. This kid has such a heart. He wants to wait for me and say goodbye. Oh, why can't he come back and hold my hand? If I could just see him one more time for him to explain he didn't want to leave and to tell me this was the way it had to be, I'd be so thankful. I don't understand why he had to go.

I wasn't there to help him, and it doesn't matter what people say to make me feel better. I imagine him calling out for me. I'm his mom. I should have been there to hold him. He shouldn't have died alone in that ambulance. If I'd been there, I wouldn't have let them take him away from me. I was always there with him when he was a baby sick with cancer. Every single day, every treatment, I was there. I never left him alone. I should have been there when he was shot too. I don't know if he was in pain or if he was scared. I don't know if he suffered.

My sadness turns to fury. I'm angry because someone made a terrible mistake that day. Shaun was only there to share some time with his brother and father. These men robbed my son of the gift of life. I am furious at the man who positioned him and the one who took his life. My anger is more than anger—I am a mother enraged at the people who killed my child. My anger increases, and the need to vomit is intense.

You didn't have to take him at that time, God. He'd just gotten married. He was happy, and that made me happy. I was so grateful that he'd survived cancer and made it to adulthood. He lived to get married and be in love with his beautiful girl. I wanted to see him have a family. He should have gone on to experience the beautiful things life could offer. I always wanted to be his mom. That couldn't come to an end.

He was a giver. He radiated kindness and compassion. On those days when I'm being selfish, and I can be, I think of him and know he would be different. I want to be more like him. He was a loving soul. Maybe that's why he was so lovely on the outside.

I touch his face and trace the smile lines around his mouth. I want to get that last precious look before they take him away from me forever. I want to hug him and feel his warm skin on my face.

I never saw him after that. It was the last time, other than the funeral, and when I saw him in the casket, I knew he wasn't there. It was horrible. But that day in the hospital, I felt that he was still with me. I thought he was watching me. I felt him hovering over his body. Was that real?

On his wedding day, I was grateful to think he'd made it this far, that he didn't die when he was little. I was proud of how he cried when Julia walked down the aisle. I saw the love in his heart. He cried because she cried, and it was beautiful. I have never seen a man cry like that at the altar, or a future wife gently wiping the tears from her future husband's face. He watched her walk down the aisle, and she was everything he had ever wanted, and he knew that she loved him too.

I wonder now if she thinks about him. I don't want his memory to haunt her, but I want her to miss him. I want her to call me out of the blue and tell me that she misses him. I know she's remarried, and I am so happy for her. And yet, could anybody ever love her as Shaun did? I was happy for what they had together, and I wanted it to last forever. There's not a greater feeling in the world than knowing your children are happy.

I don't want people to forget him. They should talk about him and bring him up in random conversations because he lived a meaningful life. This grief is such a dark place to live. I want to be a little kid again. I was a happy little girl—the one without a care in the world, the one who got her horse from the pasture and rode the trails all day. I played outside and loved the autumn leaves. Now, I hate fall because it's the season my son died. Every time I see a brightly colored leaf floating through the air on its way to the ground, or hear a crunch beneath my feet, I know what's coming. I look at the beautiful leaves and know they are dying. When they are gone and lying dead on the ground, that's when my son fell and never got up again. It breaks my heart. I'm so very sorry that I wasn't there with you, Shaun, so very sorry.

I couldn't catch my breath. I was hyperventilating. I cupped my hands over my mouth to slow my breathing, but it didn't work. I felt woozy and was afraid I would suffocate. Oh, God, what was I supposed to learn from this? Every experience in my life has taught me something. There are lessons in everything. I couldn't work out my lesson here. I wanted to start going to church again. I needed to put that back in my life. And yet, I went to church all the time, and Shaun still died. Everything feels sad in church.

I have lived through so many tragedies, but they were minuscule compared to this. Everything else was just something I had to go through. It wasn't easy, but they were nothing in comparison. Was God preparing me for this? Were all the bad things supposed to give me the strength to go through this? We'd been in so many hospital rooms, but we always came out of them together. We struggled and always made it through to the other side. Why didn't we make it out this time? I never thought God would take him from me after we'd made it this far. Why couldn't I have died along with him that day?

I don't know how to live without him. If only God would bring Shaun back, he could take me a million times over. A part of me still believes there's been a mistake and he's coming home.

I've read we reap what we sow. Even with the mistakes I made in my life, I can't believe God would take my son away. Then I thought, Blessed are those who mourn, for they will be comforted. And I tried to believe that he doesn't want me to feel that way and he forgives me. But it didn't make the hurt in my heart go away. There's that piece of me that wondered if God wants me to suffer for some reason.

I saw something the other day that said, your biggest challenge may be your greatest ministry. Every day I tell myself, "Don't feel sorry for yourself. Put on a smile and think about what you could do to help somebody else. Take it off yourself." But my heart won't let me. I feel guilty for that. And I feel so bad for my other kids. I'm worried they haven't processed it either, and it's going to affect them when they get older. They could be stuck in this grief all their lives, just like me. I don't want that to happen. I don't want to see anybody suffer this much. I keep praying that I would always have a strong relationship with them. And yet, they didn't seem to need me in their lives as Shaun did. Maybe that's because of Shaun's illness as a baby.

Each person I love has a special place in my heart. Nobody can fill another's shoes. What if I lost another son? Oh, God, please never let that happen. More voids that could never be filled. The thought sent me into another panic. I couldn't breathe. I couldn't move. I was paralyzed; I didn't know how to move forward. Will I ever move forward? What are the next six and a half years going to be like? I can't be this sad for another six years. I can't bear it. When I think about a memory from when he was little, it kills me. I want a do-over. Please, God, show me what I'm supposed to do with my life.

We continued these sessions for over a year, and each one was as grueling as I expected. Whenever I was tempted to quit, I reminded myself that the purpose of them was to let my brain process the memories and store them in a healthy way so they wouldn't stay lodged in my limbic system. Over time, I began to see an improvement. Sadness and panic still occurred, but they weren't as debilitating as before. If an image came into my mind, I faced it, breathed through it, and released it so it didn't overwhelm me and send me into a spiral of depression that would last for days. This allowed me to handle my job and daily life with some degree of normalcy.

Along with the EMDR sessions, Rick and I continued regular therapy. He helped me learn how to stop beating myself up. I worked on forgiving myself for being incapacitated by grief and emotionally unavailable to others for so many years. I learned how to love myself again. It was a tough journey, but it gave me back a life worth living.

EMDR is not for the faint of heart, but in my opinion, it is well worth it. It can be an effective method for reducing triggers and intrusive thoughts and has a proven track record. Overall, the treatment was a good choice for me. Below is a statement from my therapist, Rick Jass, MA, LPC, President of Charis Counseling, Wausau:

"EMDR is not for everyone because the process is rapid and can be intense. Cindy was a good candidate because she did not shy away from the pain and was willing to face it. Many people look to avoid their pain, and as a result, end up prolonging it and causing more problems in their life. A saying I use in therapy is: 'The way out is through.' Cindy has embraced that concept and has the courage to go through the pain from her trauma. It has been instrumental in healing amid tremendous grief and loss."

Journal Entry
February 7th, 2013
Dear Shaun,

If we could have one more day, we would go for a long walk and talk the entire day. I would want to know what heaven is like and what is going on in your world. You probably know what's going on in mine. I would share with you all the things I never had a chance to say. And you would tell me you already knew. I would watch you smile and freeze it in my memory, knowing I only had one day with you. I'm curious about where you have been throughout all this pain and sadness. You tell me you wipe my eyes and hug my heart. I tell you I didn't want you to leave. And I know the rest of this journey is mine and I must make it on my own. I know at the end of the day I have to say goodbye, hug you tight, and be grateful for our day together. Oh, if I could have one more day. There are so many things I want to say . . .

Love you,
Mom

CHAPTER EIGHTEEN

THE SHOULD'VES, WOULD'VES, AND COULD'VES

Losing you taught me to be grateful for every day.
If only I could go back and savor every moment.
—Cindy Baumann

IT WAS TIME to get back to dealing with the regrets that plagued me. The definition of the word regret is "sorrow aroused by circumstances beyond one's control or power to repair." For so long, I'd believed the more I planned, looked to the future, and stayed on top of things, the more control of my life I would have. But this was an illusion. The only thing I could control was my reaction to the things that happened.

Since I was a flawed and imperfect human being, those reactions weren't always what I wished them to be. I lived a long time in the land of regret, and I'm not alone. People have told me they screamed until they were hoarse over their regrets after a loved one died, and others went on a path of self-destruction because of the anger they felt toward themselves. A close friend told me that he had so many regrets, he could fill a book with them. When he shared this, I wanted to reach through the computer screen and hug him for his honesty.

In my case, my mind processed everything to do with Shaun over and over again in a maddening loop of second-guesses. I was suffocating under an avalanche of should'ves, would'ves, and could'ves. Why couldn't he have enjoyed a carefree childhood instead of one filled with cancer treatments? Should I have stayed in my first marriage so Shaun wouldn't have been uprooted by our custody arrangement? If only I'd been home the day he decided to go hunting—he might have skipped it and hung out with me. Had I done enough for him? Why had he endured so much only to meet such a tragic ending?

I felt I didn't have the chance to make up for something I said or did or failed to do while Shaun was alive. I tortured myself with doubts, criticisms, and questions, wondering if we had been too tough on him. I beat myself up over being too busy to be present for him and berated myself for not making one more phone call. Weighed down by the thought that I had left so much unsaid and heartsick to think I could never make it right, I spiraled downward. It seemed that a door was shut to me, and my chance to mend things was gone forever. On and on the voice in my head went, keeping me stuck in a cycle of unending grief.

The first step to freeing myself from this torment was to stop pretending that I wasn't feeling it. I had to name it and claim it before I could deal with it. I had to admit to myself that in my heart of hearts, I feared time had run out, robbing me of any chance to correct things I believed I'd done wrong. I had to face the fact that I feared that further communication with Shaun was now impossible or, at best, very limited. It was time to stop running from regret, and anyway, I had run out of places to hide.

Had I stayed withdrawn and alone with these hopeless thoughts, I never would have found the guidance and inspiration that is available through the wisdom of others. Fortunately, I had the strength to keep seeking answers from sources other than my own tortured mind. Someone who helped me greatly was the author Robert Holden, who was a frequent guest on a popular radio show. Every time I tuned in to his show, I found comfort in his message. I reached out to him by email, and he took the time to answer me in my darkest hour. Now, over ten years later, he was gracious enough to write the foreword to this book.

My two great fears were addressed by Robert in these teachings: 1) Our bonds with our loved ones are not dependent upon physical forms; therefore, those bonds are not broken when someone dies; and 2) Time never runs out, because in the world of eternity, there is no time. These concepts have become so important in my life that I want to explain each more fully here.

In Robert's email, he said, "Always remember that real communication is not between bodies—it's between minds and souls." When I read that sentence, the lights started to come on for me. I suddenly realized the closeness I had with my son was not because we were physically mother and child, but because our souls were bonded. Love was an energy that may have used human forms for expression, but it certainly wasn't dependent on those bodies for its existence. The body was secondary to the soul. This meant that our soul connection survived death. Although we cannot walk physically by each other anymore, our souls still co-exist and share experiences together. Most of all, we share love for one another.

Of course, because I am living in the world of the five senses, it's a natural instinct to want to use all those senses to communicate with him. My eyes miss looking into his eyes, my hands miss touching his hands, my ears miss hearing his voice, and so forth. But Scripture tells us that we have spiritual bodies, and I have faith that our souls use our spiritual bodies and their senses to communicate. When I tune into that part of myself that isn't dependent on physical form, I find the essence of Shaun is as near as breathing.

The second main insight I gained from Robert is that time has not run out on what I wish to say to him. My chance to express my feelings to him is not gone, only changed in form. Shaun has a wider perspective now that grants him a level of understanding he didn't have before. He can hear me or, more accurately, sense me, including my thoughts and the feelings inside my heart. My words of love are felt and reciprocated, my gratitude is appreciated, my apologies are heard and accepted, and the reasons behind any tensions we might have had are understood and forgiven. I now talk soul-to-soul with him rather than face-to-face. This concept is a practical truth in my life, not an abstract idea, and it has helped to set me free.

Another helpful source for me was Ira Byock's book, The Four Things That Matter Most: A Book about Living. Dr. Ira worked in palliative care and learned through observation what it is people want to hear and what they need to say during that stage of life. He suggested that we have real conversations with those who are dying and with those who have already died as well, focusing on the following statements:

"Please forgive me."

"I forgive you."

"Thank you."

"I love you."

When I practiced using these simple words, I found them to be incredibly powerful and healing. I said them often, asking Shaun to forgive me for where I felt I fell short, and forgiving him for leaving us so abruptly and not saying goodbye. I thanked him for all the joy and love he brought to our lives, and I said "I love you" many times over. This exercise allowed me to release some of the guilt that was festering inside me.

Another helpful technique was imagining I was sitting across from Shaun and having a conversation. In my mind, I would reach out and hold his hands before spilling my heart out. Then, I would listen for his answer. During these exercises, I truly felt connected to Shaun. I believed he could hear me, and his responses felt authentic. I knew he wanted me to go on and live my best life, to take everything I have learned about love, humility, gratitude, strength, and faith and share it with others. He let me know that he hoped I'd complete my course and fulfill my potential while I finished out my lifetime. He didn't want his death to be the reason I gave up on all that.

Using this technique wasn't a "quick fix," but over time, my grief softened. It changed me at my core and affected how I treated others. It taught me to be more present and to enjoy the magical moments of life and love. It reminded me to always say "I love you," and give that departing hug when I leave somebody. Most of all, it guided me to share what I have learned with others so they may be comforted and strengthened.

Meditation is another method for connecting with our loved ones. I figured that Shaun could reach me more easily if I could quiet my thoughts, so I decided to try meditation. During Lent, I went to a special meditation training class at our church. The priest told us that whenever our mind wandered, we should say to ourselves "Jesus," and that would bring us back into focus. This sounded encouraging, but my mind raced off after every passing thought like a puppy chasing a ball. Every few seconds I had to say, "Jesus, Jesus, Jesus." How could I empty my mind when I was constantly having to say something to myself? I concluded that my overactive mind was better suited to something else and decided to try several forms of writing instead.

First, I kept a lengthy journal throughout my grieving process. It was soothing for me to put my emotions and thoughts on paper and let them go before I fell asleep, releasing them with faith that Shaun was not judging them, but valuing them instead. Some days my entries were long, and at other times, they were very short. It wasn't necessary to put a lot of words down or to write anything profound. No matter what words I chose, I felt my heart was seen and understood.

Next, I took up soul writing, sometimes called automatic writing. I was first introduced to it in 2009 when I read Janet Conner's book, Soul Writing: How to Activate and Listen to the Extraordinary Voice Within. Soul writing turned out to be very healing for me. It started with a short meditation practice to still the mind, and then I wrote a question or a statement directed to God or to Shaun, and waited for an answer. I didn't censor myself during these exercises. I simply wrote whatever answer came to me, letting the words flow without concern for correctness or anything else. The answers were enlightening and gave me a sense of connection and peace. I continue to use this technique today, and I'm always amazed at the messages I receive.

In addition to soul writing, there are so many practical, here-and-now things that can be done to honor someone's legacy. In our case, Shaun wanted to be a doctor, so his scholarship fund helps others fulfill their educational dreams. He loved plants, so we support the botanical gardens. Because of his illness, we donate to different organizations that research or support childhood cancer. I believe he is aware of all that we are doing in his name, and he is pleased. It's as if he gets to watch the seeds of love he planted in his life blossoming into gorgeous flowers that make people smile. Tributes can be very simple too. What counts is not how elaborate the tribute is, but the power of love that flows through it.

Expressing my regrets and shortcomings to Shaun allowed me to forgive myself, get back on course, and keep rowing toward shore. I put gratitude, apology, and forgiveness in God's hands and asked Him to deliver it personally to Shaun. I knew Shaun wanted me happy, for when I'm happy, I am more useful to God's plan of healing and uplifting the world.

One of my friends told me that before she goes to sleep, she tells God to take the good things about her day and use them to help her loved ones who have passed on—or anybody else that needs a boost of loving energy. I love this idea and try to do the same. Knowing that happiness is a gift to share, I've made the conscious decision to dedicate my moments of laughter and smiles to Shaun's memory. I offer up the energy and goodness that is generated in my happy moments for him to use for his spiritual benefit. I had to remember that if I were in heaven and he was on Earth, I wouldn't want him to wallow in regret. I would want him to go on and live a beautiful life for his happiness and in my honor.

In the end, I realized that it's a deeper expression of my love for him to release regret and live a productive life than to stay mired in my sorrow. I believe Shaun let go of his baggage before he left this world, and he only took love with him. I want to be a reflection of that love on Earth.

The longest life is just a breath in the span of eternal life, and the shortest life may have the greatest impact. When I looked at death from this perspective, I could see that Shaun's passing was part of his spiritual journey, and because we loved him, it's part of ours as well. Full understanding will remain a mystery until the day I die, but while I am here, surrounded by the real needs of people around me, I can dedicate myself to the mission of being a light in the darkness to the best of my ability.

Nothing can block the power of love. Not death, not the lack of a human body, and not time itself. My conscious mind may be busy with the tasks of physical life, but my soul is still laughing, communicating, and creating wonderful experiences with my son. I'm content to know this is going on whether I can see it happening or not, for I know the time will come when we will be together in the same place.

Here are some samples of my soul writing letters to God and to Shaun:

Dear Shaun,
    Please talk to me . . .

From Shaun:
    Mom, what I want to say is hard. I love you and I know how much you're hurting. I want things to be better for all of you. Soon it will be. Until then, keep your head up and keep trying even when the days are hard. I miss you too, and yet I'm with you. You were my buddy too, Mom, and you will always be. We are connected through love. Please try and understand this world is brief. My world is forever and beautiful. God is wonderful . . . keep believing. Someday this will make sense. I know losing me was hard. The winter is especially difficult. Go someplace warm and get outside. Feel the sun. It's beautiful.

    I know you feel like a mess, but you aren't. Don't be so critical. Everyone means well. Find joy in everything you do; it will help you heal. Writing your book is a good tool. People will like your book. Don't wait for a miracle. It will happen as you're writing. It will come together. Be in peace. Learn to love life and remember I'm always with you.

    I love you, Mom, more than you'll ever know. Just because I'm not there doesn't mean I love you less. Why did I leave all of you on that day? I didn't know it was going to happen. I was feeling funny but didn't know why. Sorry I never called you or said goodbye. I know that has been hard on you. I'm okay. I am. Everything happened so fast. I didn't feel a thing, but I was scared. I yelled out for you.

Please, Mom, don't cry. I know you miss me. Soon—I promise. Until then, live. I will hold you again. I visit you, but you don't know it. And the pennies are from me, all of them. There's more to come. Just keep watching and don't give up hope. I'm here. I can't physically visit you. There are rules that I can't break—even for you. Please know how much I love you. Now, start writing your book.

Shauner (Bud)

***

Dear God,
Teach me how to feel Shaun around me.

From God:
Cindy, Open up, be aware, feel, love, be present. Trust. Share. Slow down. Shaun is everywhere. So am I.

***

I also wrote a letter listing everything I struggled with and apologized for the areas where I fell short in the past. When I was finished, I said a closing prayer and burned the letter. This symbolized that my thoughts and feelings weren't dependent on a piece of paper and that God heard me no matter what form my prayers took. It helped to leave my regrets in the past where they belonged and seek new ways of living life that are aligned with my ideals.

Regrets kept me trapped in my grief until I learned how to address them. I must admit it took several attempts and a lot of forgiveness before I was able to let go of the guilt and start to embrace happiness. Gary Roe, an author, chaplain, and grief counselor, shared this quote that really resonated with me: "Guilt is not your friend. It helps no one. It doesn't help you live well, grieve well, honor your child, or love the people around you. When it comes knocking, just show it the door."

It took time, but thank God I didn't give up in coming to a place where I could express gratitude for the time we had with Shaun and then turn to the present, confident that I will see him again. I had to practice patience and be kind with myself—this was a process. And in the middle of it all, God was there.

In time, I came to terms with it. I wished his life could have been easier, and I know I loved that kid with my whole heart. I adored everything about him, and he knows that. I clung to the fact that even though I couldn't protect him from the pain in his life, he lived and died knowing his mother loved him.

CHAPTER NINETEEN

THE MANY FACES OF GRIEF

If you can't fly, then run. If you can't run, then walk.
If you can't walk, then crawl. But whatever you do,
You have to keep moving forward.
—Martin Luther King Jr.

ON THAT TERRIFYING day I cut my wrist, I sensed God saying that I would find peace on the other side of ultimate loss—and I have. It goes without saying that it's been a gradual process, not a quick fix. Each morning when I arise and hear the birds singing, I'm so thankful that I had the support and inner strength necessary to persevere. I know that when the time comes for me to leave this world, I can do so knowing I didn't give up and add another layer of loss to the lives of my loved ones by committing suicide. I know that I've given something to Shaun that he would have wanted from me—a spirit of gratitude for the gift of life.

Like others on their journey, I went through many faces of grief: shock, denial, disbelief, sadness, abandonment, confusion, guilt, regret, anger, hopelessness, loneliness, bargaining, anxiety, fear, depression, nostalgia, emptiness, and finally a form of acceptance. My progression through these emotions was all over the board. I've learned that it's normal to bounce between them, sometimes even many years later, and it's normal for the edges to overlap. This is true of many human emotions, and grief is no different.

My experience of shock, denial, and disbelief was exactly as you may expect—I didn't believe Shaun had died, and I didn't want to interact with other people. I'd held Shaun's lifeless body in my arms, but I couldn't accept that it had happened. It was a nightmare from which I'd wake up. I thought some kind of miracle was going to happen, allowing Shaun to reappear. I could see it in my mind's eye—he would walk through the door one day, whole and healthy, and the constant heartache I was living with would end.

Along with this came the desire to withdraw from life in general. I wanted nothing to do with the world or any of its activities. This was a 180-degree change for me, as I'd always been an extrovert, eager to be a part of whatever was happening. Now, nothing that I loved to do before interested me, and I had no energy for conversation. It took every bit of strength I had to put one foot in front of the other. My life force was all wrapped up in surviving. I guess disbelief and denial are the natural, protective reactions of our minds when trauma occurs, designed to shield us from shock, but being in this chronic state of shock is physically and mentally exhausting, and can leave us unable to participate in life.

Anxiety, hopelessness, and anger bewildered me with their intensity. I was incredibly angry—at God, the shooter, and even at Shaun. His guardian angels must have been on vacation that day. Otherwise, they would have whispered in Shaun's ear to bend down and tie his hiking boot, or given him a push. They were sleeping on the job, and I wanted nothing to do with a heavenly Father who didn't protect his children. I'd always been able to find comfort in prayer and church, but now I shut the door to God, and anything associated with him. The faith I relied on faded when I needed it most and my life felt hopeless.

Just as God and his angels had been negligent, the shooter was in the same category. He didn't kill Shaun intentionally, but he could have prevented it. I couldn't forgive him. Even the thought of letting him off the hook felt like a betrayal of my son. My anger was part of my love and loyalty to Shaun.

I was shocked when I experienced anger not only at the shooter, but at Shaun. But there it was—the idea that he betrayed me, that maybe he had a choice whether to live or die and had chosen to leave me. I was angry and bitter at the world. I experienced outbursts of anger where I sent my grieving emotions in other directions; otherwise, they would have overwhelmed me.

Amid all this, I attempted to bargain and make a deal with God. Even as I rejected him, I needed him to supernaturally change what happened. I tried to deal with God, saying, "If you will please bring my son back, I will live an honorable life, one that you will be proud of. If you just bring him back, I won't tell a soul. I'll hide him from the world and keep what you did for me a secret." I alternated between shutting out God and praying to him for a miracle. Occasionally, I still spend time negotiating with God, but in a much different way. Now, I beg him to allow Shaun to show me signs that he walks with me. I ask him to fill my heart with the Holy Spirit so I can touch and heal people around me. The grief of others is so real to me, and I want to make a difference wherever I can.

The feeling of hopelessness morphed into fear and depression, which hit me hard and lasted a long time. I'd pull out of it for a while and then it would return. I didn't want to get out of bed and found no pleasure in the things I enjoyed. The thought of never feeling joy, excitement, or happiness again terrified me. I'd always had a zest for life, and losing that resilient side of me was frightening. I didn't recognize myself. The Cindy I knew was fun-loving, enthusiastic, supportive and energetic. Without those traits, my identity was gone. This was the period when I almost gave up on life, sometimes in practical terms and sometimes in theory. I was disappointed that I hadn't died in my sleep. At night I would say the prayer that my parents taught me as a child:

Now I lay me down to sleep
I pray the Lord, my soul to keep
If I should die before I wake
I pray the Lord, my soul to take.

I wanted God to take my soul home. This world was too heartless for me to live in. But he had other plans for me.

These various emotions would come on suddenly, and even after they'd eased up, they would return. As time passed, other experiences occupied my attention and consumed my energy. I became desperate to "put my load down," and once I came to terms with a form of accepting what happened to Shaun's physical body and understanding that his spiritual presence was still with me, life started to open back up.

Accepting and understanding that Shaun had died didn't mean I felt it was justified. It just meant I acknowledged what happened and admitted there was nothing I could do to change it. I didn't have the power to stop the bullet that killed my son, but I have power in the here and now to create a meaningful moment. Whether that means appreciating the warm sunlight or sharing a smile with a stranger, I get to choose what to make of my time—and that's an incredible gift. When we learn the value of the present, the space in our mind that was filled with all these painful emotions starts to empty, leaving space for other experiences.

To achieve that emptiness, there were things I had to release. I let go of the dream that God would grant me a special favor and reverse the events of that tragic day. I let go of the hope that Shaun could return. I acknowledged that the shooter was a flawed human being who had made a terrible mistake of judgment and was suffering because of it. Forgiveness didn't come overnight, but understanding was the first step toward it. When I reached that place of release, I felt a sense of peace. I did it for Shaun, but in the end, I was the one who benefited. I sincerely hope the man who shot my son has been able to forgive himself and find a way to contribute to others. If you are struggling to forgive, understand that it may take time. Don't try to rush it, or it won't be authentic. When it blossoms in your heart, you'll know it is real.

As things shifted, the needs of my other children and family members became a priority again, and I also yearned to be available to my friends. They'd given me immeasurable help, and I was grateful beyond words to them. I was eager to give back to everyone who'd helped me. I wanted to contribute something of value. I thought about the saying, "Service is the price you pay for the space you occupy." I knew this stage was going to be tough, but at some point, I had to come to terms with what had happened and live again.

Life is brief. Before I know it, mine will end. There is much to do and so many people to learn from. I pray God will send me more grandchildren, so I may feel the sweetness and potential of their precious lives. I know Shaun will have met them before they come and will have blessed them with a kind, loving heart, just like he did my granddaughter Braelynn. I want to be an example of inspiration and positivity to them as they grow, and I know I need to work on developing and sustaining these qualities in myself.

None of the processes is easy. There will always be something empty inside me. But now, when bouts of grief wash over me, they are shorter and less intense, and I have effective tools to cope with them when they come. My life is better because I worked hard to get to where I am. I'd rather have loved than have only experienced things on the surface.

I'll always live with a degree of anxiety and fear. Loving others means worrying about them, but there's only so much we can do. We're not in control of everything. We can do our part, then we must turn everything over to a power that is vaster than we can comprehend. This act of turning things over and giving ourselves permission to completely feel and grieve will help us move forward.

Everyone's grief journey is unique—you may experience some of these emotions or many more. You may be confused or disorganized as you walk through the healing process, or you may revisit some of your feelings many times over. It's important to be as gentle with ourselves as we would be with a friend who is suffering. We need to learn to take our advice regarding self-care. We live in bodies that were created by God; it's right that we respect them. We need to walk on into the future with hope and courage.

You may find moments of happiness occurring out of the blue and feel guilty about it. I remember the first time I felt a flash of happiness. We were out with friends, and I laughed. In addition to getting a reassuring look from friends that I was back, I could almost hear Shaun cheering. He wanted me to be my fun-loving self again and was glad I'd turned a corner. Just like he'd been with me through all my emotions of grief, he was with me in moments of happiness too. I can honestly say that no matter how dark things became, I always felt the presence of Shaun's spirit.

Another strong emotion associated with grief is nostalgia, and I was no different in this. Some people struggle to let go of a house or piece of property that is connected to their loved one. I experienced this when we decided to sell our home in 2015. In a way, I felt like I was abandoning Shaun. We had built a garage up north a few miles away from our old cabin and later converted it to a cabin as well. When we decided to sell our family home and move into the cabin, I was upset. As much as I wanted to leave this house and not be surrounded by Shaun everywhere I turned, it was difficult to go through with the move. As the boxes and furniture left the house, I walked into each room and sat in silence remembering the beautiful times we shared. Tears ran down my face and I questioned whether it was the right thing to do. It may sound strange, but I was afraid if I left there, I wouldn't feel his spirit with me anymore. As I drove to the cabin following the moving truck, I begged Shaun to make the move with us.

I had to work hard to make peace with the decision by telling myself it was a temporary move. We were going to live in the cabin until we figured out what was next in our life. I soon discovered that Shaun did move with us that day. He is an eternal part of us, and we carry him in our hearts no matter where we go. As Saint John Chrysostom said, "They whom we love and lost are no longer where they were before. They are now wherever we are." I don't have to be in a certain place to feel a connection to my son. He is within me and around me, not dependent on a body or a location. After five years, we are still living in the cabin and plan to stay. Life is simpler for us here, and I know Shaun would be happy for us.

It took me a long time, but I finally learned that it's important to allow yourself to feel grief. I wish I would have taken more time to sit in the closet with my face buried in a pillow and feel my grief, rather than trying to run from it. You truly do need to feel in order to heal. Grief is a journey that none of us wants to be on, and yet there's no turning back. The only way out is forward and through. You must walk down the path and try to figure out how to integrate your loss with your life. The lack of your loved one's presence will always be part of your life. It's a case of learning to balance the two. It's a process, but I've found that our reaction to our losses changes over time. More than anything, this is what I want my story to convey. I also hope to empower others to share the wisdom they've gained after going through the process of grief.

CHAPTER TWENTY

REACHING THE OTHER SHORE

I now know the true meaning of love, and I would
never give up the opportunity to have loved you.
—Cindy Baumann

JUST AS I was starting to see the shore on the other side of grief, my brother Terry died of a heart attack. He'd just turned fifty-six and was in perfect health. My first reaction was to ask the question "Why?" He and his wife, Valerie, had raised four fantastic children. They'd recently been blessed with their first grandson, and my brother enjoyed every minute with that little guy. He gave his love wholeheartedly to his beautiful family. Now, they had to live without their husband, father, and grandfather.

Terry's contagious smile lit up our world, and he had the best belly laugh you've ever heard. He was never too busy to help. He had a heart of gold. I remember the times when he would stop by after a long day on the road. We would laugh about silly things, happy just to be together for a while. He was a good, compassionate man and his passing was a huge loss to many people. My brother touched countless lives, and will be deeply missed, especially by his family, mom and dad, a house full of sisters, and all his brothers-in-law, who were his best friends.

Grief hit hard again, but this time I had something to fall back on. I dug into my repertoire of healing tools and did some soul writing. I wrote one letter to God and one to Terry. In this letter exchange, I sensed God telling me my brother was finished with his experiences on Earth and that his life had come to completion. He explained that it's to be expected that we're grieving his loss, but that Terry is happy and at peace. He said there was a place for me next to my son, and that I would be next. The thought of that is both comforting and concerning, especially when the struggles of life are exhausting. He said life is all about learning to expand our capacity to receive and give love.

In my letters with God, I felt him saying it's all about lessons in love. God suggested in this letter that I worry less—good luck with that one. Don't worry. Trust in the Lord. Today, I try to release the fear that makes me think I can protect everybody and turn it over to the one who is in charge. Notice I say the word *try*— I fail regularly, but I'll get there.

Here is some of Terry's letter to me: "I tried to save my life when I felt the heart attack coming on, but I saw it was time, and I accepted it. So, I let go. There was nothing anyone could have done. I didn't suffer, and I'm at peace. Don't get caught up in the world. Live each day. God sees your struggles and knows it's hard on you and everyone else. I'm with Shaun; everything is perfect and beautiful here. I'm sorry I had to leave and put everyone through this. Life can be so crazy. But this was meant to be. It's a part of the plan. It will get easier. Just let go and trust in it. Shaun sends his love and hugs. I, too, wish we had more time to talk, but that's life on Earth. Take care, Sis. I love and miss you. Be the strength of tomorrow."

Those last words mean so much to me. I want to live in the hope of a beautiful tomorrow, for that will give me the strength to love the day I have today, instead of yearning for the days gone by. I have to remind myself that "for now, we see only a reflection as in a mirror; then we shall see face to face" (1 Corinthians 13:12).

Going through the shock and pain of losing a child gives a person unique insight into grief that we can use to help others. When Terry died, I was grateful to have some understanding to draw from. I was able to share what I learned with my parents coping with grief, who lived as I do with the incredible sadness of losing a child. They are both in their eighties, and I knew how hard this experience was for them. My dad is an introvert and would sit alone with his sadness while my mother struggled in her own way. I sensed that they were ready to let go of life and join their son. I talked with them about it and begged them to hold on a while for the rest of us. I let them know that their lives have value and how much we need them.

I also took my mom to a grief group I led at our church. I passed on the strength I gained through therapy and experience and reminded them that Shaun and Terry are together, enjoying each other and guiding the rest of us on our journey home. This belief and our faith in the hope of unity helps us all feel at peace.

Sharing your wisdom doesn't have to come in the form mine did. You might be moved to make a call, send a card, put up a post, or simply give a grieving person a hug. I learned from losing Shaun that these kind gestures mean the world to someone when their heart is breaking, and I hope I never forget that important lesson.

It took a while to accept the blessings in my life that exist beyond the dark clouds. Finding myself again after losing my identity seemed like an endless journey. Everything I believed about myself changed the day I lost my son. I had to find a new me, and I didn't want to. Slowly, though, a new awareness of the sweetness of life began to filter back into my heart. I felt the warmth of the sun on my face. I noticed the smell of fresh dryer sheets on a crisp fall morning. I enjoyed the newness of spring, the heat of summer, and the scents of fall. I could see the depth of the bright blue in the sky and the striking colors of a sunset. Once my awareness of these things was awakened, my senses were more intense than ever before. I'd taken so much for granted and had been in such a rush during my goal-oriented phase of life. Now I know how quickly things can change, and I value each moment, person, and experience.

They say time heals everything. I think instead that time softens the scars, but it doesn't completely heal. I compare it to a physical injury. Although we may be able to use the injured part of the body again, there may always be a twinge of pain—and that's okay. I don't fight those twinges anymore, and yet I don't let them stop me from cherishing the life I have.

Throughout my years of grief, I was searching for magic fairy dust that would make my sorrow go away, or at least help me understand why this happened to Shaun. I wanted to find a shortcut through my grief to avoid facing the reality of the loss. I looked everywhere, reading books and listening to and talking with people. I learned that there is no such thing as magic dust, but there are some lasting truths that I can rely on if I open my heart and listen.

As I have re-entered life, it's clear that I'm different. People told me that something good would come from this. Honestly, I never wanted to hear those words, but as I noticed my bitterness softening and my heart opening up again, I knew it was true. Ultimately, I've become a better person. I had to deliberately choose this outcome, though. I could have stayed out in the middle of the river in a state of bitterness and sadness, teetering at the edge of the whirlpool. It wasn't until I made the conscious decision to become fully engaged in life that I saw the silver lining in the clouds of grief. I had to quit living with one foot on Earth and the other in heaven and stop wishing I could die. I had to recommit to life with my whole self, not just half of me. Here are some of the ways I've grown from the experience of losing Shaun:

CLEARER PRIORITIES

One of the most important changes came in the form of a shift in my priorities. Before losing Shaun, my career consumed me. Now, I take more time for my family and for myself. I'm grateful for all the beautiful people God has placed in my life, and all the little things as well—the flowers in the garden, the bird singing in the tree, the sound of laughing children, and most of all, spending time with my family. These are the things that light me up inside.

I no longer desire the big, beautiful house. I prefer a smaller, comfortable home. After two house fires and then Shaun's death, I've learned that things can be replaced but people can't. When the kids and grandkids come to visit, I want us to be crowded and close together. Their visits are the highlight of my world; they are what is truly important. I couldn't love them any more than I do. Every minute we have together is so incredibly special. When my boys are here with me, I memorize the moments as I watch them interacting, and I listen to them laughing and talking. The same is true of my daughter-in-law, Maria. She is like one of my own. God bless her for loving us as she does and for being the mother of my granddaughter, Braelynn.

Jordan recently got married, and his lovely wife, Chelsea, has graced our life as well. It's wonderful to see the love shining in their eyes and watch them remodeling their first house together. And Justin, the baby (he hates it when I call him that), is busy following his dreams and building his own life and he is seriously involved with someone as well. If it takes me any longer to write this book, she may also be an addition to our family. I wish my future daughters-in-law and grandchildren could have met Shaun, but

I know as we tell stories about him, they will get a sense of what he gave us in his short life.

Along with prioritizing my loved ones, I prioritize myself. I take time to go for walks, to take classes, and to be with friends. I don't work endless hours at the office anymore. I've created a part-time, manageable workload. I've learned that I can't give to others what I don't have to give myself, so I recharge as I need to through reading, walking, writing, art, and meditation—yes, I finally mastered it.

I expanded my knitting capabilities and learned to make sweaters and tried my hand at the sewing machine. My mom is such a great seamstress, so I hoped I'd have a knack for sewing, but I found it took more patience than I possess—at least at this point in my life. I also tackled the art of stained glass, which was a challenge and a delight, but I discovered that painting is the best fit for me. Abstract art in particular seems to match my personality. Seeing those colors swirl about on the canvas is a good way to release my pent-up emotions. When I paint, I get lost in time, and I usually end up with paint all over me. I am a messy artist! Sometimes, I feel Shaun watching me, and I feel so happy to share the energy of my creativity and happiness with him. I have found being creative and dabbling in art to be good therapy.

In this way, I've learned to lead a balanced life—a balance between giving and receiving, relaxing and working, socializing and retreating, creating and resting, doing and just being. I wish I'd learned how to slow down earlier in life, but from conversations I've had with people, sometimes it takes heartache to teach us these things. A deeper appreciation for balance also comes with age. I look back at my younger years and see how I missed so much by always being in a hurry. I jumped into the rat race without giving a thought to how else I might do things. I'm so thankful that I am no longer caught up in that way of living. Quality over quantity, that's my motto nowadays.

LIVING IN THE NOW

When I was a child, I would wake up in the morning, stare out of my bedroom window, and watch the tall pine tree sway in the wind against the bright blue sky. I'd wonder what I would do on this perfect day, and would jump up eagerly, ready to find out. I'd have a bowl of Rice Krispies sprinkled with sugar as I held my kitty on my lap, chattering and bickering with my sisters and brother as we sat around the table. We would each have a box of cereal in front of us and pretend we were reading the back of it, but the truth was, at times we just wanted to avoid each other. Growing up with three sisters and a brother in our house was hectic, and there was never any alone time. Next, I'd get on my bike and ride in the sunshine on a quiet back road to a nearby pond and walk through the cool water. I felt so alive when I was outside with the trees, almost like I was part of them and could feel their energy. The world was like an open book, full of endless opportunities ahead of me.

I didn't realize it, but I was living in "the present moment." This is a phrase that has become commonplace—but to me, it's forever new. It means seeing the value of who, what, and where I am right now. It's recognizing that in any given moment there is a particular combination of things that will never come again in precisely the same way. Things might happen again in a similar way, but they can never be identical. Something will be slightly different, from the blades of grass growing a millimeter more, to the shifting tides of the sea. It's treasuring the song of the birds at sunrise, sitting with my husband on the deck watching the hummingbirds, and feeling the breeze blowing from the north. There is no part of our existence that can be captured, preserved, or reproduced. This is why each moment is so amazing—it's literally one of a kind.

Shaun knew how to live in the moment. Whenever he spent time with one of his brothers, he was 100 percent present. He never multi-tasked or gave a piece of himself. He gave his all—mind, body, and soul—to whomever he was with. You felt special when he looked into your eyes and spoke to you, because he wasn't distracted or preoccupied. Maybe he knew in his soul that he needed to make the most of the time he had left.

But what about the rest of us? We have no idea when we'll exit our bodies and say goodbye to this world. Shouldn't we all live as if we are dying, as if *now* is all we know we have for sure?

Each morning I try to remember to ask myself, *What do I want to make of this moment?* Because this moment leads to this hour, this day, this year, this life. I know if I can do that, when I get to the end of my life, I'll have a stream of awesome present moments woven into the fabric of my being. I'd like to bring a stream like that home to God and Shaun. I'd like to say, "Here are some beautiful experiences, and I was present for each of them." I want them to see I used my suffering as fuel for the fire of personal growth.

It would be great to go back in time with all the wisdom I have gained through my life. Maybe there is a dimension where that is possible, but for now, I am living in human time, and it is always marching forward. Everything on Earth is temporary. So much of the sorrow we experience in life is because we pretend to ourselves it isn't so. I can't control the fact that I live in a temporary condition, but I have spent a tremendous amount of my precious time trying to.

Thank goodness we don't see what is ahead of us—each day we are granted a new start. I will always miss my life and the old me—the mother of four wonderful, living sons—but I have accepted those days belong to a phase of my life that has passed.

I'm the first to admit grief can block me from being aware of the present moment. Sometimes my mind goes back to that horrible day, but thank God, it's less frequent than before. When it happens, I feel Shaun catch me when I fall, and then I sense him helping me stand back up. I think between God and Shaun, I have a dynamic team cheering me on. I realize that when I live in the present, I'm not leaving Shaun behind—I'm taking him with me.

Shaun once gave me this message through one of my intuitive friends: "Don't let what happened chew you up and spit you out. Make it count for something." That's what I'm focused on. If I can help another person get through their grief by being a good listener and sharing what I've learned, I believe I will have done just that.

GREATER COMPASSION FOR OTHERS

It seems to me that this whole world is a big school, and the #1 course of study is Compassion. One person's pain is another person's opportunity to exercise compassion. I hope I never forget this important lesson. I've learned that when your heart is breaking, kind gestures mean the world. I've also learned that being helpful to other people is one of the greatest forms of therapy. Compassion may take the form of a simple gesture, such as sending a card or giving someone a hug, or it may be the privilege of walking beside someone for months or years as they navigate the wilderness of grief. Never doubt the power of the smallest act of kindness. Take the time to follow that hunch or make that call. It might save someone's life.

Someone shared this story with me that captures the power of compassion: A life coach once received a call from a man so desperately sad, he believed there was no purpose to life. He said he was ready to kill himself if he didn't see a reason to stay alive. The coach told him to go outside and walk until he saw something he could do for somebody else, no matter how small it was. The caller did what he was told, and soon noticed the dirty front porch of an elderly neighbor's house. He picked up a broom and swept the porch. When he was finished, something had changed in him. He was acutely aware that he was surrounded by people who needed a hand. What greater purpose could there be in life than to offer his assistance? He had been healed by the simple act of helping somebody.

Everybody is carrying their hurts inside, some worse than my own. Recognizing this fact has helped me to be more sensitive and less critical. When I hear of a tragedy, my heart fills with compassion for those involved. Things are no longer happening to somebody else; I know they can happen to any of us. When I hear about a child who has died, I pray for Shaun to take care of them and to send comfort to the ones who have been left to grieve. I believe he was there the day of the terrible Sandy Hook Elementary School shooting in 2012. He would be the kind of soul God would send on such an assignment. He held all those children in his arms so they wouldn't be afraid and led them home.

God created us to live in connection. He gave us one another so we could take turns being weak and strong. I was broken beyond description and had to lean on the shoulders of others. Now, it's my turn to hold someone up. I try to remember that appearances can be deceiving—someone can look as if they're functioning on the outside while they are crumbling on the inside. A word of encouragement may be what they need to make it through another day. I want to be part of that.

In general, I've become more respectful of all living things. The sight or sound of a gun is upsetting to me, and I don't even want to see an insect killed. If I find one in the house, I try to capture it and set it free outside. They are living creatures and have a mother too.

Part of being compassionate means being vulnerable to the heartache that can accompany love. I know that the depth of my grief is a reflection of the immeasurable love I had for my son. For years after he died, my heart was afraid to love. I wanted to protect myself from the possibility of losing somebody else and going through the same intense heartache. Even today, I dread losing my grief dogs who are now fourteen years old. They have been there beside me as I've shared a million tears, especially Sami, and I know my heart will break even further when I lose them. I don't ever want to give them up, but I know that time must come. Even though I know that impermanence is built into everything in the material world, I would always choose to give and receive love rather than to reject it. I try to keep an open heart to whomever I meet, wherever I go.

APPRECIATING THE KINDNESS OF OTHERS

I finally began to understand that God had been with me all along—not in the way I'd expected, but in the faces of my friends. The word *grateful* is not enough to express how I feel about the many acts of kindness that were done for me. There were so many, I could never describe them all. One was from a client—or more accurately, a friend—named Mark. He kept me from crawling under my desk and wishing the world would go away. He helped me find the will to work, making trips from Detroit to meet about projects, even though we spent a lot of time at Starbucks. We'd sit on comfy big chairs in the corner of the shop out of sight from everyone so I could hide the expected tears. I'd have a cappuccino with a hint of chocolate, and he'd have a strong cup of coffee as he asked questions about how I was doing. He understood and never expected me to "get over it." He sent me links to sermons that he thought would strengthen my faith and always let me know he was there if I needed him. Mark was a gift from God sent to see me through. He was an inspiration; I cherish what he did for me.

Another friend whose loyalty never wavered was Pam. I saved the cards I received through those years, and there were a whole lot signed by her. She remembered every event, whether it was an anniversary, Mother's Day, a birthday, or a holiday. She never gave up on me, whether I responded to her or not. People have busy schedules, and when somebody goes out of their way to remember you, it's clear that God is present. I will never forget how God worked through my special friends. I recognize them as one of the main components that helped me heal.

There are countless other people God put in my path as well. Without them, I'm not sure what would have become of me. They never let me quit, even in my darkest hour. The unexpected encounters made the difference between surviving and ending my life. Family members, friends, acquaintances, and strangers—God sent them all at the right time.

These beautiful people have no idea how much they helped me with a small gesture or thoughtful words. While they couldn't remove my sorrow, they never gave up on me. I understand this is how God works—we are his hands when we reach out to others with love. God manifested himself through the people who loved me. This helped me realize that if he was with me, he was surely with Shaun as well. I have no reason to fear for my son. He is in the very best hands, the kindest hands of all, the loving hands of God.

DEVELOPING A DEEPER FAITH

Rebuilding my faith was the most powerful component in my journey out of the darkness. I'd avoided church for years, but when my son Justin asked me to attend Mass at his high school, I didn't want to disappoint him. He thought the different surroundings would make it easier for me to sit through the service, but unfortunately, I did the usual amount of crying. To spare him seeing my tear-streaked face, I tried to leave as soon as the service ended, but he dashed up behind me, calling, "Thanks for coming, Mom." In that moment, I recognized that God was using Justin's powerful faith to reach through the walls I'd built around my soul. It was time for me to attend my church again, for my own sake and the sake of my family.

My return to God was a gradual process, like the unfolding of a flower, and well worth the wait. I met with my priest, and he advised me to pray specifically for help in managing my paralyzing grief. I prayed and prayed until my mind collapsed and God took over. I felt the frantic pace of my thoughts give way to his stillness, allowing me to once again regard God as the author of truth and goodness rather than the author of suffering. I was reminded of a saying I'd heard before: "If you don't feel close to God anymore, guess who moved?" I could feel myself turning back to God rather than turning against him, seeing how he'd never left my side, even though I'd left him.

One of my friends told me she believes that the Earth is a workout gym for the soul. Adversity may strengthen our spiritual muscles, but God sprinkles in the determination needed to keep going. He provides hope so that even after we've been wounded, we can open our hearts again. If we lean into him, we will find in his welcoming arms the strength to live again.

GRIEF'S KISSES

Grief took so much away from me along the way, and yet it graced me with a gift I call grief's kisses. This kiss is so soft, at first I couldn't feel it. Once

I became sensitive enough to recognize it, though, I felt it as the tenderest treasure. In all these kisses, I can feel Shaun's love. Without a doubt, he was one of my great teachers on Earth. He was nonjudgmental, unselfish, and loving, and patience came naturally to him. He taught me what was important in life, and I will forever be grateful for what he gave me. Today, it's my goal to take the gifts he brought and do my part to make the world a better place.

Some say this life is a big classroom where we can study the lessons we were sent here to master as well as teach others the ones we've completed. There are a multitude of things out there that I haven't figured out, and until I do, I know I'm here in this Earth School to learn them. I want to graduate from the classes God has enrolled me in and grow in wisdom before my time comes to leave.

As I enter my sixties, I look back at what the world has taught me, and I am grateful to have reached the point I'm at. I find purpose and meaning in each day because I know that tomorrow is not promised. I'm learning not to live in the past or the future, but in the only thing I know for sure—the present, with its limitless possibilities. Today, I'm ready to branch out into new adventures.

I have always loved learning, so I'm continuing to take classes and expand my knowledge of the world around me. Spirituality and grief are on the top of my lists of interest. I plan to dive deep into my life-coaching career, helping people move forward in their grief. And I will make plenty of time for art days with my mom and sisters. When we get together and work with color, the days fly by. We are immersed in the joy of the moment and love creating unique pieces. I don't know what else will come into my life as I explore these new adventures, but I pray this book will be part of that outreach. I want to convey to my readers: You can do this. Don't give up. Life on the other side of grief can be beautiful and joyful again.

I know I have a purpose, and I want to fulfill it. Of course, I would give up all the lessons I've learned to have my son back. It has been an unfortunate experience, but I'm determined to make the best of it. The alternative is to waste the years I have left frozen by grief, and what is the point in that? I don't want to get to the end of this road only to be filled with regret because I let the gift of life slip by. Even though tragedy has touched me many times, I cherish my time on Earth.

Death is a mystery, and I've come to accept that it's a natural part of life. Acceptance means just that . . . I know I can't change it, but I don't have to like it. When we face mortality, our existence becomes much more beautiful, because we no longer take it for granted. I once heard, "If the ending to something is tragic, that means you haven't reached the real ending." I've given a lot of thought to that. When we go through terrible things, we assume that's the end of the story, which plunges us into despair, but we are forgetting it is only a chapter in a story that ends in love and joy because that is the ultimate plan of God. This means there is much more to the story of Shaun's life and mine. I just can't see it yet. We have the beautiful gift of life in front of us. I invite you to embrace it to its fullest.

Just as I was finishing this book, I received a dear message from Shaun delivered through a gifted spiritual friend:

> I want my mother to know that everything she is doing with her life is equivalent to watering the seeds I planted while I was there. When somebody dies, the seeds they left behind can be cultivated into a beautiful garden, but only if somebody else takes the helm and finishes the growing. Even if the person has left behind seeds of anger and sadness, they can be recycled in a sense, transformed into fertilizer to make good things grow.
>
> It makes me happy to see her cultivating what I left, and it connects me to her, as it would if we were working together to design a real garden. She's growing my garden for me and I'm along for the ride! I get to watch, but I help too, by offering ideas in the form of thoughts and giving general support. I sit by her as she works at her computer and help her feel the right connections.
>
> Those who pass over do the same thing from this side of existence. The seeds she planted in me—seeds of love, patience, humor, faith, and generosity—are the ones I've brought here. I planted the seeds, and everybody admires the flowers that are blooming. That's what the gardens of heaven are made of— the seeds within our souls that we plant when we come here. The gardens here go into Infinity, and they have tiny plants you can barely see right up to shrubs and massive trees that stretch beyond our vision. They are made of the colors of Earth and the unworldly colors of heaven. I want her to know the seeds she planted are here and thriving, and they are really something amazing to see!
>
> Some people don't have much to bring with them, but God helps them if they arrive with less to work with. I'm so fortunate to have brought so much with me. I left a lot of seeds on Earth too. It's my legacy. But it could have faded away if my family had not taken care of

the life garden I'd started. My mom supports me here and I support her there. Neither of us has any reason to feel separated. Our souls don't need bodies to communicate and share experiences together. I hope she will think about this as she goes forward. I hope she feels me with her when she gets tired. She's growing the garden of love that I didn't have time to finish and teaching other people that they can do the same. Wow! I mean, just wow! I love you so much, Mom.

When days are gray, I stop and visualize the colors of those flowers and trees in Shaun's garden, reaching high into infinity. If the colors of heaven are beyond what we know here, surely the love we have on Earth is faint in comparison to the intensity of love in heaven. I imagine an aspect of myself sitting in that garden with him, while the part of my soul that has more work to do here in this world keeps forging ahead . . . and I feel at peace.

Today, my feet are planted in warm sand on the shore of the other side of the river of grief. I am fully embracing all that life has to offer, but I often look back and remember my voyage and pray for those who are still in its waters. I hope this book raises a beacon of hope they can see to guide them to safe harbors, so they will know they are not alone.

Journal Entry
July 15, 2019

Today I feel I can make it and be happy again.

CHAPTER TWENTY-ONE

IN THE WORDS
OF OTHERS

*The most beautiful people we have known are those who have known
defeat, known suffering, known struggle, known loss, and have found
their way out of those depths.*
—Elisabeth Kübler-Ross

WE ALL CROSS the river of grief at our own pace and in our own manner. Our experiences are as different as we are and as unique as the individuals we have loved and lost. Below you will find some thoughts from other grieving parents who have lost a child. I hope you can find some nuggets of strength and wisdom in their words.

JACK, DAVID'S FATHER: LOST SON AT AGE SEVENTEEN TO SUICIDE

What helped most in healing your grief?
Unquestionably, friends and family who understood my grief and shared in it. There is nothing that could be said or done, except for those individuals who were there to console and listen to memories. The true nature of family and close real friends shines at times like these. There were times that I just needed to be alone and not have people trying to cheer me up. Those that understood that were the best.

How has grief changed you?
I guess I learned to grieve a long time ago when I lost my older brother to a car accident and then my father to heart disease. Being a medic in the service and then a hospital administrator, I saw and experienced a lot of death. You start to become immune to the grief, but when it is your own child, much is different. But dealing with the grief is the same. I internalized it and dealt with it and decided my life would go on without those loved ones.

What has grief taught you?
That life is precious and to be lived to its fullest. We exist to have memories, not to be consumed by them. The future is for the living and the past is for those who did not survive. In God's grace we may all be united again sometime.

What regrets did you have regarding your loved one and how did you overcome them?
So many regrets it would fill a book, but the main one was that I didn't recognize early enough my son's struggles with Asperger's. I also regret that the school administrators, counselors, and therapists were not informed enough to recognize his problems and to assist him in overcoming them. I live with the failures I had as a parent always and can only hope that I give some sense of purpose to my remaining family.

How has your life changed since the loss?
I have moved on and remarried to a loving and supportive spouse. I choose to remember my son as he was and may have been, without letting it control me to act differently than I would have if he were still alive and with me.

What advice could you pass on to other grieving parents?
Everyone grieves differently. Don't listen to the BS that the one who died is in a better place. That is just total BS. His or her place was better off here on Earth with us. Realize that if it was suicide, it is the ultimate selfish act because it accomplishes nothing but to leave the people that person loved behind in misery.

Have you tried any healing therapies or techniques to help you heal?
None whatsoever. My memories and power of positive thinking are my therapies.

Is there anything else you would like to add?
I just pray that when I die, I have left behind a legacy of happiness and joy for all those I have known and loved. I really believe the old saying that in every personal encounter, one should try to leave those they have met in a better place.

JANELLE: DAVID'S MOTHER, LOST SON AT AGE SEVENTEEN TO SUICIDE

What helped most in healing your grief?
Time is the only thing that has helped me, although it's been ten years and I still feel the pain of my son's loss.

How has grief changed you?
Still have an underlying feeling of loss. There are almost daily reminders, both good and bad, that trigger some sadness.

What has grief taught you?
To appreciate the people and things in my life today, as nothing is permanent and it can be gone tomorrow.

What regrets did you have regarding your loved one and how did you overcome them?
I have too many regrets to list. I live with them daily but try not to think about them.

How has your life changed since the loss?
I made a physical move away from the city where I raised my son. It's easier for me to live somewhere where there are fewer memories. I also have reduced contact with some of the people that I knew then. It's easier to be with people that don't know my history.

What advice could you pass on to other grieving parents?
Not sure, it's an individual journey. There is no right or wrong way to grieve.

Have you tried any healing therapies or techniques to help you heal?
I joined a few support groups, but after a few meetings, discontinued. Mostly because it was too "early" to share my story. Also, there were a few people in both groups that had been attending the group for over ten years and I found that too depressing, so I stopped attending. I did a few sessions with a therapist but didn't feel that helped me. My feeling is that nothing really helps much, nothing will bring my son back, it's just something I have to live with.

I do what I call "beach meditation," walking or just sitting, smelling the sea air and watching the waves. It's a place my son would love and is very calming. I enjoy traveling, as did my son, and in the past several years I started taking a handful of his ashes and distributing them in various places in the world. In the past few years, he's "traveled" with me to New Zealand, the Danube River, Quebec, Canada, and the Mediterranean Sea. I usually say a little prayer or have a little "conversation" with him when I toss his ashes into the air or sea.

Is there anything else you would like to add?
Not really. I have a lot of "good" in my life and really appreciate it. However, I don't think one ever gets over the loss of a loved one, especially one's child. It becomes a part of them.

ROSANNA, HANSEL'S MOTHER: LOST SON AT AGE TWENTY-ONE IN A TRAIN ACCIDENT

What helped most in healing your grief?
The first night after Hans died, I instinctively told myself, as if in a survival mode, if I were going to survive this (and by survive, I mean to find joy in my life once again), I had to be grateful for what I had. So I started to make sure I counted my blessings every night. I bought vitamins and slept as soon as I could to forget. I collected quotes and put them in my pocket, and asked people for fun movies to watch. Ironically, all funny movies seem to involve a funeral. I made sure when my husband was driving with his eyes in the clouds, my eyes were on the road not to have mishaps. It helped to have someone that felt my pain as intensely as I did.

I read so many books trying to find answers and bring peace. *Healing After Loss* by Martha Hickman and *Tear Soup* by Pat Schwiebert and Chuck Deklyen have excellent verbiage and helped tremendously. *Wokini* by Billy Mills gave me strength. *Now* by Eckert Tolle taught me the value of mental health in living in the present. Books helped, but beyond a doubt family and friends and yes even especially strangers. Where was God in all this? I am not a real religious person, but I do believe in a higher power beyond our understanding, and this higher power works and speaks to us through living things.

Never have I felt the sacredness or closeness of God so powerfully as when so many people surrounded my family with an outpouring of love and compassion. Simple kindness was more healing than one can imagine. Someone brought me a cup of tea on my break at work one day, that same person called me, on the night Hansel died, while on her way to an appointment and left me a message. A stranger wrote me a letter to tell me that after losing her son, her happiness eventually returned. Such hope! I clung to those words of encouragement.

Another person called me to say her son called and said he loved her. What comfort that gave me to have her share this with me. A friend went square dancing with me for two seasons and that truly helped. I would highly recommend it because it is teamwork that requires constantly listening and responding, the human touch is healing, and the music is joyful. Time . . . time helps teach one to cope, and after a couple of years I finally said and I meant it for real, "Okay, I will try to accept it." Then the peace flooded over me.

Immersing myself in work and keeping busy helped me live in the moment and gave me focus. Working, walking, being outdoors was healing for me.

How has grief changed you?

Grief has, I hope, made me a more open, compassionate person. So many parents have lost a child. I discovered I did not lose my identity like I thought I had initially. When I admitted to negative feelings, they eventually dissipated after acknowledging it. So I no longer get jealous seeing some mother with her son. I am stronger, surviving this, than I thought possible. I chose life, and I didn't think I wanted to ever make that choice. I've met people and have become friends with strangers through my family's loss. I have learned I am not in control, so I worry less but pray more.

I try to laugh more and to enjoy my time here on Earth as being a very precious gift.

What has grief taught you?
I am so touched by so many good people on Earth. We all suffer losses of one kind or another—we just don't know when it is going to happen, do we? I looked, begged, searched, and pleaded for signs for the longest time. Once, on my way to work, I saw sun dogs in the sky and a comet arched in front of me as I said the words, "He was but a brief moment on Earth." Another time, I came home to find a tree to plant. Maybe they were signs of Hansel, maybe not, but they certainly were signs of a beautiful world we shouldn't miss. Grief has taught me not to worry so much. You can't change a thing. One realizes we all have life's disappointments, and another's problems are often much greater than our own. Grief has helped me be more open to others' suffering.

What regrets did you have regarding your loved one and how did you overcome them?
Here come the tears. I have many regrets I could dwell on, but I cannot re-write history and have to concentrate on moving forward instead. I would have not sweated the "small stuff" trying to raise him. I regret I didn't tell him more what a wonderful kid he was, joke more, apologize more when needed. When Hans died, I was so upset I could not have been there to be with him, yet I had some interesting things happen that week beyond my understanding, so that was my blessing and I have to have hope because otherwise there is despair. And I believe there is a higher power of good we all gravitate toward even when we hit rock bottom. I believe in Jesus's message of forgiveness. Forgiving yourself is hardest.

Have you tried any healing therapies or techniques to help you heal?
At first, I saw psychics and searched desperately for answers and wanted to know he was all right. A pastor welcomed me often to her grief group; she too had lost a young child. I couldn't go. I felt I had nothing to offer and would be overwhelmed by trying to listen to another person's sorrow. A neighborhood tree planting ceremony, remembering his birthday, making gifts out of his clothes are all drops in the bucket, but the drops all add up. For me and its personal for all of us how we deal with our grief, but it was being busy, that became my plan. Learning new things even on a small

scale gave me a sense of control and calmness, and renewed interest in life. I am so grateful for so many kind ways people have reached out to me. They became my teacher in their examples. Sending cards, notes, books as a way of reaching to others when people reached out to me in that same way. Giving back in some way eased my own grief. We cherish our memories of Hans, new stories are like gold nuggets.

What advice could you pass on to other grieving parents?
It's important and necessary to grieve. At some point a seed will be planted and you will experience a moment of joy and a sense of normalcy. At first it may be brief, that happiness or calmness, but it will continue to grow until there is a tipping point and you will experience more joy than sorrow. Don't despair, hang in there. Have faith, be patient with yourself.

TAMARA, DEMETRIUS'S MOTHER:
HER SON ENDED HIS LIFE AT AGE TWENTY-THREE

What was it that helped you most to heal your grief?
After my son died, I had no one to talk to that was able to listen. I found journaling was to be my lifeline. I had my notebook with me at all times, and I used it to pour out my thoughts, feelings, fears, worries, impressions, lightbulb moments, dreams, and anything that arrived in my new awareness, at any moment.

Journaling enabled me to lean into my grief. I learned that the more I could be fully present with whatever my grief was showing me, the more I would move through it and get to another side of my feelings. I became more familiar, more watchful, more willing to experience my life head-on. I could actually feel myself healing, growing, and knowing myself better than ever before.

Your journal can be a gauge as time passes, a sort of compass, outlet, and reminder. I suggest you date/time your entries, so as you experience, you can refer back to when you wore two different color socks to work and see clearly that you are no longer wearing your slippers to grocery shop (yes, I did). You will be able to re-read your entries and know that you are making progress in your grief. So write about your dreams, sadness, anger, and even joy. What works for you, what does not? Write about memories; tell stories, wishes, and what you miss; and don't miss. Your journal will help you to realize that you truly are living life and your grief is a major part of your life. This eventually became a technique that I share with others as a grief coach and have since 2004.

What has your grief taught you?

My grief has been my greatest teacher in life. I learned that all we have, really, is right now. And everything, the good and the difficult, is temporary. Everything is temporary—and also an opportunity to see the world with different eyes. So, I used my grief to motivate me. I have learned to worry far less about outcomes and focus on the moments. I have many regrets, but the biggest and most ugly regrets stem from having not jumped into action when my heart was telling me to speak, to act, to help, to make that call, and to give. So, I allow my sense of guilt to be my best motivator, to get off the couch, grab my phone, make the call, make the connection, reflect the mirror for someone, say the words that come from authenticity, gratitude, compassion, and love.

How has grief changed you?

The day my son died, as he was lying still . . . I was having a quiet lunch with myself, and feeling so grateful for the life I have. Healthy kids, happy life. When I learned of my son's death later that day, I knew that nothing would ever be the same ever again. That was true.

I also could not have known that the gift of loss and his death gave me an opportunity to deepen, to view the world with different eyes. I felt an instantaneous change in perspective and realized the things that used to be important no longer would be ever again. I found a compassion for others unlike before, I learned to listened more deeply, and I spoke with fewer words and more significance. I looked in all things for the significance. It is my deepening that is the gift of the depth of my love for and from my loved ones.

It takes you there, if you let it . . . and it is now mine. I hope I never have to give it back. It has now been twenty-four years since he died. I never could have imagined in 1996, having to live through twenty-four days let alone twenty-four years without him in my world.

If I can offer a thought now, this far down the road . . .

There will come in time, a natural moving beyond the paralysis of grief. You may hesitate to allow it, so let it come slow, at your own pace; it can come in small steps. We resist the moving on because we feel we might be betraying our love for them. No way.

We will not and cannot ever forget them! And we are not betraying our love if we laugh, have peace, move to a new city, eat our favorite food instead of theirs. We are supposed to keep growing, becoming, and changing, and our love for them goes along with us; they will be part of us and who we are forever. Let life move through you, live it large, and they will be happy for you. Of this I am certain.

What has helped you to heal?
I quickly realized that if I don't take care of myself as I work through my sorrow, there could be little left of me. So, I learned to take "grief breaks." These breaks became an oasis for me.

I made sure I had a massage every week. It served to regenerate me and connected my mind, body and soul. I meditated to become more grounded and focused and to quiet my mind, hush my thoughts. I consciously/actively simplified my world. We work so very hard to continue our lives as they were, but when you are grieving the death of your loved one, it is impossible. So, give yourself permission to be where you are and make room for your grief in your world.

Allow someone else to host the Thanksgiving dinner, bake the pies. I let someone else drive the carpool or help in the classroom. I had to stop volunteering myself. Doing this allowed me to be present with my grief as it would arise. With four children, I was far more present with them. Simplifying, saying no for now to the busy activities, felt far healthier than trying to keep up with my other life. It is exhausting when you are grieving. I healed when I gave myself room to be quiet, to remember, to be still in between the busy day-to-day stuff.

One thing that helped my entire family:
I found it to be enormously helpful to talk with my family about the calendar of events as the date of the anniversary, or his birthday, or holidays are approaching. We feel this approach coming but can't always name it until it is upon us, like a big surprise. So, watch the calendar, and two weeks or a month before the big day, have a family chat and make a plan: How do we want to approach the day? An example, on the first time it was his birthday after he had died, we all agreed that we would make his favorite cake and decorate it in a fun crazy fashion.

We did. And the younger kids picked the colors and too many sprinkles and stars . . . and then . . . we allowed for the spontaneous fun. When

I was serving the cake, it flipped out of my hands and onto the table. So, I picked it up and ate it with my hands, everyone flipped their cake onto the table, and we ate it with our hands, feeding it to each other and laughing hysterically. A very solemn day became a day we always remember with a big smile. Prepare for the difficult days and make them your own. Together, have a plan, be spontaneous, and bring your loved one along.

Healing yourself after such a major impact as the death of a child or loved one is the hardest work you will ever have to endure in life. My children lovingly pointed out to me many years ago that they know they can handle anything life hands them because they have lived through the death of their brother and learned so, so much. I am beyond proud of them.

NAN AND GARY, CHAD'S PARENTS: LOST THEIR SON AT AGE TWENTY-ONE TO SUICIDE

What helped most in healing your grief?
- Letting God in
- Continued learning about grief
- Sharing and helping others—very important for us

How has grief changed you?
Everyone is changed by grief, whether or not you want to be. It readjusts your life assumptions (example: don't assume you will die before your child), resets your priorities, and allows you to focus on what's most important in life. I hope that it has made me more compassionate and less judgmental. I truly have a heart for people and their hurts and wish I could take away their pain. I found a purpose and meaning that gives me "spirit" every day.

What has grief taught you?
- Dream of tomorrow. Everyone has to have dreams and goals, but don't be disappointed if they don't turn out as planned. That trip to Florida can be just as rewarding as going to Australia.
- Live for today. Be grateful for what you have. Someone else doesn't have it this good!
- Friends and family relationships change. That's not a bad thing, just an adjustment.
- Life is full of ups and downs, disappointments, failures, and trauma. This was not the first and would not be the last. Expect that things will happen again.

What regrets did you have regarding your loved one and how did you overcome them?

No regrets. Life and death happen. Chad didn't mean to hurt us. If any regret, it would have been that I wish I could have changed things, but it wasn't meant to be.

My biggest "pain" was knowing I would never be a grandmother. Prior to Chad's death, I dreamed of that day. Losing that dream has been a sorrow I always carry.

How has your life changed since the loss?

Changed the direction of my career. It wasn't about making money anymore. It was about feeding my soul and living the best life I could after devastating loss. I've met wonderful people and unbelievable friends around the world—yes, literally. Each has added to my life and made me realize that I am just a small part of a greater experience.

What advice could you pass on to other grieving parents?

Hang in there. Be patient with your grief. Don't let others minimize your loss or shame you into thinking you have to "get over it." Take time but learn how to let go. You can't move forward when you forever live in the past. You can honor the past—your loved one's life—in other ways without hanging on to the "Why me?"

Have you tried any healing therapies or techniques to help you heal?

This is individual preference, and all of them can work. Gary and I called it our "quest." We tried many different things, usually for short periods of time, and then went on to the next. Some work. Some don't. It really comes down to your inner spirit and your relationship with your God and your support system that help you get through it.

For me, writing was my greatest "tool" for healing. I have written articles and other things since I was a teen. Writing about my grief always brought out the emotions I was feeling and soothed my soul. I'm grateful that I've been given the ability to use written words, because the spoken ones still raise the emotion in my soul.

. . .

KATIE, TAYLOR'S MOTHER:
LOST DAUGHTER AT 5 MONTHS OLD TO SIDS

What helped most in healing your grief?

One hundred percent, the most helpful thing was that we were surrounded by so many friends and family. They showed up every day for months to the point that we had to leave town to be alone. We put up pictures of Taylor all over our house to make sure her memory was everywhere we could turn.

How has grief changed you?

For the longest time I didn't want to be away from my husband or my kids. I definitely appreciate the time I have with them more than I think I ever would've. Over time we got back to socializing, but it's different for sure.

What has grief taught you?

Compassion and grace, I would say, are the two biggest things that I learned. Watching Mark and I go through grief so differently has really helped me to be supportive of others that go through loss. It's given me an understanding that no two people grieve the same.

What regrets did you have regarding your loved one and how did you overcome them?

We went to an event the day before Taylor died and did not spend the day with her. It took us a long time to be able to socialize away from home. That was definitely part of the grief process and forgiving ourselves for not being there with her on her last day alive.

How has your life changed since the loss?

So many things changed. I changed jobs. Mark had opened a running store business and has since closed it. We now realize we want to spend more time with family again and that we now have something to lose, trying to run a small business, versus after losing her we had nothing to lose.

What advice could you pass on to other grieving parents?

Don't be afraid to talk about your child whenever and wherever you want. Remind people that it's okay for them to say her name. Lean on people and don't be afraid to ask for help. And most importantly, be kind to yourself.

There are days when it's okay if you don't want to get out of bed and days where you feel great, and that's okay too.

Have you tried any healing therapies or techniques to help you heal?
We've done a lot of things. I did the rapid eye movement to get past some of the initial trauma that we had. Obviously, community and doing fundraisers in her memory like Team Taylor has been the biggest one. I still sleep with her stuffed monkey and we include it in our family pictures every year. We spend lunch on her birthday and her angel day at her gravesite every year also. Supporting other families is healing in its own way.

MARK, BRANDON'S FATHER: LOST SON AT AGE EIGHTEEN TO A SEVERE ASTHMA ATTACK WHILE CLIMBING THE MOUNTAINS BEHIND THEIR HOME IN SCOTTSDALE, ARIZONA

What helped most in healing your grief?
It was a combination of things, not just a single thing. I call these my "5 pillars of healing grief":

- Support from family and friends.
- Building relationships with others who've been through the same thing.
- Service: Giving to and helping others helps you heal.
- Forgiveness: This includes forgiving yourself and letting go of feelings of guilt.
- Being open to afterlife evidence: Our children and other loved ones do continue on after physical death. For me and many parents I know, this was the most healing, but it needs to be accompanied by the other pillars as well.*

*Afterlife evidence includes direct experience, or reading/hearing the accounts, of others, related to the following phenomena: Spirit communication (evidential mediumship), near-death experiences, death-bed visions, induced after-death communications, reincarnation research, etc.

How has grief changed you?
It made me re-examine my life and my priorities. I shifted from an unbalanced focus on work and career to placing primary importance on family, friends, and relationships.

What has grief taught you?
This life is short, and you need to make the most of it. We each have a purpose, so take time for deep contemplation to discover your path and then follow it. Love a lot, share a lot, and live a lot.

What regrets did you have regarding your loved one and how did you overcome them?
Like many parents who experience the passing of a child, I sometimes thought that I could have done something more to prevent it from happening. In most cases, that's simply not the case. One must realize that you can't control everything and it's okay to let go of things that hold you back.

How has your life changed since the loss?
Although I miss the physical presence of my son Brandon very much, my life today actually has more depth, meaning, and sense of purpose. We are all here to serve in some way; it's incumbent upon us to examine ourselves and figure out how we can best serve.

What advice could you pass on to other grieving parents?
Refer to my "5 Pillars of Healing Grief" above. They also need to be patient with themselves, allowing time to feel better. It's okay to cry when you feel like it. No matter one's level of faith and belief, the grief process cannot be circumvented.

Have you tried any healing therapies or techniques to help you heal?
- Prayer.
- Body work.
- Reiki.
- Meditation.
- Membership in a grief support group. I'm actually the co-founder and chairman of the board of Helping Parents Heal, which now has 15,000 members and 90 affiliate chapters worldwide (https://www.helpingparentsheal.org).

- Working in a field related to your loved one.
- Creating something (memorial, event, art piece, music, garden) to honor loved ones.

STEPHANIE, EVAN'S MOTHER: LOST SON AT AGE EIGHTEEN TO SUICIDE

What helped most in healing your grief?
Nan and Gary's support group. Specifically, it was a place to express my feelings, where others could relate, and I was especially encouraged by seeing Nan and Gary happy and okay. It gave me hope that healing was possible. Same with Compassionate Friends, even though I only went a couple of times. There were people there who had lost children thirty years before and they were laughing and smiling.

How has grief changed you?
Overall, I am a much more compassionate person than I used to be. I'm more in touch with my feelings—not just the negative, but the positive ones too. My faith in a higher power has expanded beyond one religion's teachings and is more real than it ever was before.

What has grief taught you?
Life is precious. Healing requires feeling one's feelings, no matter what they are. I can survive things I never would have believed I could.

What regrets did you have regarding your loved one and how did you overcome them?
Mostly, I regretted that I hadn't been able to save my son from the mental illness that took his life. I should have been more on top of it, gotten him better or different help, etc. I overcame it when I realized that I am not a god and I can't and don't know everything. I am a human being doing the best I can at any given moment. Evan made his own choices, independent of me. His path and my path did cross, but his path was ultimately his own.

How has your life changed since the loss?
It wasn't the case at first, of course, but I'm in a much better place than I ever was before Evan's death. The biggest changes are that I quit drinking, got out of my unhealthy marriage, became a life coach, finished college,

and moved from Wisconsin to Seattle, and even wrote a memoir called *Backbone*. I am happier and living a life that I think he'd be proud of.

What advice could you pass on to other grieving parents?
Feel and express your feelings without judgment, seek support, and have compassion for yourself and take care of yourself in the same way you would a good friend.

Have you tried any healing therapies or techniques to help you heal?
Yoga, support group, manage a charitable fund in Evan's name at the Community Foundation, journaling, writing poetry, hypnosis, reading spiritual books (especially on the afterlife and personal growth).

How did these therapies help you?
I think every single thing I did played some part in my healing, though the support group, journaling, and writing poetry stand out as the most important to me.

Is there anything else you would like to add?
Evan has been gone for almost fourteen years, and I think it's important for those early in their grief to look to others further along the path for inspiration and hope but not to compare themselves.

SUE, KYLE'S MOTHER: LOST SON AT AGE SEVENTEEN TO A CAR ACCIDENT

What helped most in healing your grief?
The words and deeds of family and friends. Dan and I leaned on each other a lot. Friends learned as time went on how to help—how to treat you normally when that is what you needed and when to let you cry when that is what you needed. Good friends and close friends. Family gave you permission to have fun and try to keep on living. Time also helps.

How has grief changed you?
I find it hard to find complete joy in anything. There are times that the thoughts get tucked into the back of your brain and you have fun, but it doesn't take long to think that someone else should be here enjoying it with you or being out there enjoying their own life.

What has grief taught you?

How to treat and hopefully help others that are going through it. Also, you never know what life is going to throw at you and to treasure what you have and who you have.

What regrets did you have regarding your loved one and how did you overcome them?

We had taken Meagan to college that Friday, and we got caught up with all that entailed and didn't get to Kyle's football game that night. He passed on Sunday. I regret that he is not here, but I can never overcome that.

How has your life changed since the loss?

It changed who I was as a person and the level of joy I could feel. I know how it makes me not always present because I am lost in memories. I am sure others could tell you more how I have changed.

What advice could you pass on to other grieving parents?

Don't be afraid or ashamed of any feelings you have. You are in shock and you will go thru multitudes of emotions and thoughts—some you will not be proud of. Also, when people want to help you, take it. You need the help and your friends and family want to help. Also, ask others for help with jobs that are too hard to do. We asked family to help us address and send the hundreds of thank-you cards that Dan and I wrote out. Also, someone came and asked what they could do, and we asked them to mow the lawn. It wasn't a huge thing, but we needed it and they felt that they could help us. People will also say things to you that they think are helping and they are really off base with their comments. Remember, they usually don't know what to say and they just want you to know that they care.

Have you tried any healing therapies or techniques to help you heal?

I went to a few grief support meetings and spoke to my medical doctor about it. I sought help at church and in prayer. As you know, we started a scholarship and have golf tournaments. It is a wonderful feeling to see family and friends come together for a day and have fun in Kyle's name. It also is very healing to be able to give out scholarships to kids to help with their education. Lastly, Dan and I volunteer quite a bit, but I don't think that is out of grief. One more thing, when someone locally, that I know on some level, loses a son or daughter, I feel compelled to go and see them and talk about what they are going through. I hope it helps them.

Is there anything else you would like to add?
I know that I am not the only person to lose a child and that many other people have had far worse experiences than me. For that I am grateful, but my grief is still a heavy burden and very personal.

DAN, KYLE'S FATHER: LOST SON AT AGE SEVENTEEN TO CAR ACCIDENT

What helped most in healing your grief?
Sue and I leaned on each other and supported each other, and prayer and friends. Family tried to help, but many times it seemed like they tried to heal you the way they felt you should heal. Sometimes it felt they didn't understand where you were, and their "solutions" were either something you were not ready for or they didn't understand your mindset.

How has grief changed you?
I think it just made me quieter and more reflective.

What has grief taught you?
Appreciate every day you have with your loved ones and don't get caught up in little things.

What regrets did you have regarding your loved one and how did you overcome them?
Regret not spending more time fishing with Kyle and doing other things with him. Regret not listening better. Some regrets have not been overcome.

How has your life changed since the loss?
I appreciate the loved ones I still have.

What advice could you pass on to other grieving parents?
You *can* get through this. Don't give up. Don't forget that others who miss that person are also grieving. Time heals.

Have you tried any healing therapies or techniques to help you heal?
Prayer is the most important thing. You can turn to God, and he is the one that can lead you through. I went to grief counseling a few times. We started the Kyle Kempen Memorial Golf Tournament over ten years ago. Sue has worked extremely hard on this. The tournament has been therapeutic for us because many, many of Kyle's friends, their families, and our relatives have supported it. We are able to laugh, reminisce, and celebrate Kyle's life and the great memories that each of us have had with him. The scholarship has raised money that has helped many Bruce High School students with college expenses. Also, this is an athletic scholarship and students are required to provide an essay on what sportsmanship has taught them in their young lives. We see many qualities that Kyle possessed in these young students.

BRIAN, SHAYNA'S FATHER: LOST DAUGHTER AT AGE FIFTEEN TO A SUDDEN UNEXPLAINED CARDIAC EVENT

What helped most in healing your grief?
Finding a new perspective on what death is.

How has grief changed you?
Grief has caused me to re-examine everything, eventually leading to a new career.

What has grief taught you?
That human beings are more resilient than we know.

What regrets did you have regarding your loved one and how did you overcome them?
None.

How has your life changed since the loss?
I now live in service to others, and I no longer fear death.

What advice could you pass on to other grieving parents?
You can heal even if you don't believe it, even if you don't want to.

Have you tried any healing therapies or techniques to help you heal?
- I have meditated daily for the past four years.
- Attended three grief counseling visits.
- Became a member, affiliate leader, and board member in a grief support group, Helping Parents Heal.
- I am a grief guide and life coach.

PAIGE, BRYAN'S MOTHER: LOST SON AT AGE TWENTY-THREE WHEN HE WAS BRUTALLY MURDERED

What helped most in healing your grief?
By far, the one thing that helped me the most was embarking on my spiritual journey. Without the hope that my son still lived, without the hope that I could still have a relationship with him, there would have been nothing left for me. That hope kept me alive, kept me going day after day after day. My hope turned into a cautious optimism, which eventually turned into a solid belief in the afterlife. A belief that my son still lived. A belief that we could, and do, still have an active, day-to-day, loving relationship.

How has grief changed you?
Oh, in so many ways! I am generally more tolerant of others and their chosen lifestyles. I understand now that we each walk our own path, that we are each doing the best we can do. I care less about material things; I value family and nature more than ever before. I am more of a loner now—less social—and I am okay with that. I am not afraid of dying anymore. And perhaps more importantly, I'm not afraid to express my beliefs.

What has grief taught you?
My grief and my son have been my greatest teachers. I have learned so much about life and death, and the choices we make as humans and as soul beings. I have learned the importance of sharing with others, of giving as much of myself as I can to help others heal. Grief has taught me all this, and more. Perhaps the greatest thing that grief taught me was who I am. Surprisingly, my grief journey led me to myself—to who I really am—at my core, at a soul level. And I like me now much more than I liked me before.

What regrets did you have regarding your loved one and how did you overcome them?
I have no regrets. I can't. There is no room in healing for regret. When I understood fully that Bryan is spirit now and that I am also spirit, I understood that there can be no guilt, no blame, no shame, no regret. Only love. There is only love.

How has your life changed since the loss?
Much has changed, and yet nothing has changed. My husband and I are closer, he is all I have in the physical now. We live in the same house where we raised our children. Bryan's room is a guest bedroom now. My relationship with Bryan has changed, of course, yet it continues still. In some ways we are closer than before. I "see" him every day now, I talk to him every day, he helps me with my work. Our house is still his house too; everyone that comes through the door knows this. In spite of his physical death, he is very much still a part of our lives.

What advice could you pass on to other grieving parents?
Please don't give up. Hang in there, keep putting one foot in front of the other, as much as you can. Be a spiritual seeker, the knowledge you gain will fuel you when your grief threatens to run you down. Find someone to walk the journey with, to share all your new beliefs with. Talk to your child, write down what you hear them say. Have no regret. Seek to find them as they are now and continue your relationship with them.

Have you tried any healing therapies or techniques to help you heal?
Reiki, pranic healing, meditation, psychic development, mediumship development, nature/hiking, mediums, life purpose readings, numerology, astrology, EFT, past life regression, crystal healing, body work, grief counseling, leading a support group, teaching other parents, creating many memorials, scholarship fund (for two years).

Did any of the above help you, and if so, how?
They all helped me. When I needed it most, the next healing step would present itself to me. All divinely orchestrated, divinely led. Meditation is probably the #1 tool that helped me learn to breathe, calm my spirit, and connect with my son.

WENDY, ABBY'S MOM: LOST DAUGHTER AT AGE FIVE AFTER A 4.5-MONTH BATTLE WITH LEUKEMIA

What helped most in healing your grief?

Does one ever truly "heal" from grief? Months and years pass, the frenetic pace of life continues, time seemingly softens the indescribably deep and unrelenting pain. And then, nineteen years later, while on a walk on a quiet country road, reflecting on the suffering she endured and her final days/moments of life on Earth, the floodgates open wide as if it were all happening in that moment.

My faith has been the biggest factor in "living with" my grief. God has shown himself so clearly, there is no doubt he is and has been right there with us while every single tear fell. The comfort and peace he provides is beyond any human understanding. Knowing Abby is home and safe in the presence of our heavenly Father, and the anticipation of one day being reunited for all eternity, brings a spark of hope like none other. That is likely the closest I'll ever come to being healed.

How has grief changed you?

Life, and grief, since Abby passed has likely changed me in ways I will never realize. Who would any of us be today had Abby grown up to be a now twenty-four-year-old, healthy young woman? A question that has no answer.

If any good can come as a result of such trauma, I hope grief has opened my eyes to the suffering and struggles of others and has inspired me to be more compassionate and giving, and to treat life as the fragile gift that it is.

What has grief taught you?

Grief has simply taught me that the deepest, darkest kind of pain is a result of having loved, and been loved, so intensely.

What regrets did you have regarding your loved one and how did you overcome them?

Abby was loved unconditionally by her dad and I, her six older siblings, and many other special family members and friends. If I could have a do-over, though, I would take more time to just be still, to look deep into her eyes and really listen to every word she was speaking and every thought she was trying to form. And then I would stay there as long as possible.

How has your life changed since the loss?

After years of endurance biking while raising money for cancer research and patient aid, I've come to love and crave exercise, a gift I attribute to Abby. It is my "asphalt therapy" and keeps the lifelong battle with depression at bay. My focus is on God and being grateful for the simple joys and many blessings of family and friends. I treasure any time spent with Abby's amazing siblings who have grown to be adults I respect and admire, and who make life worthwhile. They are my reason for being.

What advice could you pass on to other grieving parents?

I've never been too good at advice and will just say that we don't know what struggles others are dealing with; always best to be gentle and kind. Maybe most importantly with yourself. It's okay to not always be okay. You feel what you feel, even if it's different from what other grieving parents feel or if it's different from what others "think" you should feel.

Have you tried any healing therapies or techniques to help you heal?

In the months and years following Abby's death, our family honored her memory in many personal and private ways as well as the following:

- Participated in Families of Children With Cancer support group
- Attended grief counseling
- Made a CD filled with songs that were special to Abby and that provided comfort
- Attended Camp H.O.P.E. (Helping Others' Pain End) where two of Abby's older siblings eventually became counselors themselves
- Joined the Leukemia and Lymphoma Society's "Team in Training" program, and for seven years, completed century bike rides while raising money for cancer research and patient aid
- Organized numerous events as part of our fundraising efforts including putting on "Concert for an Angel" and a children's songwriting workshop at our area high school
- Started an annual community bike event known as Tour de Fest

Notably, one of Abby's older sisters earned her PhD in clinical psychology, specializing in psychosocial oncology. She currently develops psychosocial interventions and provides clinical services for patients with a cancer diagnosis.

Although not realized at the time, while we threw ourselves into all of these endeavors, the broken pieces of our lives were being put together bit by bit, and life was beginning to take on a new shape.

The imprint left on our hearts by one so small can only be described with one word . . . LOVE

REV. RIDDLEY, MATT'S FATHER: LOST SON AT AGE TWENTY-SEVEN TO A DRUG OVERDOSE

What helped most in healing your grief?
Spending focused time on meditating about personal memories of my son, Matt. Good events that were one-on-one encounters. Accessing and appropriating my faith basics of encountering and dealing with life.

How has grief changed you?
It has made me ultimately more sensitive to the deep grief of others by identifying the various levels of grief.

What has grief taught you?
That there are many ways to deal with grief. The sudden death of my son led me to observe some unorthodox approaches to grief by my daughters. At first I was rather judgmental, but after preparing to lead a grief group, I realized my judgment was wrong. Sometimes grief was like a tsunami for me, and at other times a continuous slapping of a wave on my face.

What regrets did you have regarding your loved one and how did you overcome them?
I spent a lot of time away from him relative to the demands of my work. Therefore, finding adequate time was challenging. I also have regrets that my acceptance of our personality differences were not totally in the open. There are some things that I wish were spoken and not assumed. The problem with death is that there are no more second chances.

How did you overcome some of these feelings?
A personal understanding of universal forgiveness, as in combining divine and human forgiveness.

How has your life changed since the loss?
There are periods of indescribable loneliness for my son. Also a desire to do things personally that I think he would enjoy and be pleased with.

What advice would you give to other grieving parents?
Seek all forms of grief education, information, and support from multiple sources. Inadequacy is a tough way to approach the difficult requirements of a healthy existence after the death of a child. Seek to be informed and loved.

Have you tried any healing therapies or techniques to help you heal?
Membership in a grief group. Leadership of a grief group required preparation and learning from the other participants. It is life changing when you're in need of it.

GARY, GRIEF SPECIALIST: LOST HIS FATHER TO A HEART ATTACK AND HIS MOTHER TO MENTAL ILLNESS WHEN HE WAS FIFTEEN

What helped most in healing your grief?
Journaling and writing. And of course, talking and sharing with others. Having "grief mentors" was huge for me. Counselors, pastors, authors.

How has grief changed you?
My losses have shaped my life, the way I think, talk, and live. So much of life is about overcoming. Loss gives us a chance to learn how to do that, and do it well. If we're willing to learn, we can come through a loss living with more purpose and meaning than ever before.

What has grief taught you?
Whoops. I guess I just answered that above. Add to that: Grief has taught me to live more in the moment—in the now—rather than existing in the past or the future.

What regrets did you have regarding your loved one and how did you overcome them?
I journaled a lot about this. I visualized them in front of me, apologized, asked forgiveness, and said everything I wanted to say that I didn't get to. Doing this over time led to a lot of healing and resolution for me.

How has your life changed since the loss?
It's never about one loss, of course. Each loss triggers all the others back there and you get to process them again, in new ways. I believe I am more peaceful and joyful now. I believe I'm learning to live above my circumstances and not so much in them.

What advice could you pass on to other grieving people?
Be very kind to yourself. Release all guilt. Guilt is not your friend. It helps no one. It doesn't help you live well, grieve well, honor your child, or love the people around you. When it comes knocking, just show it out the door. Be very patient with yourself. Grief is not a checklist to be worked through. It's a heart process that is more like a winding journey through uncharted territory.

Have you tried any healing therapies or techniques to help you heal?
- Prayer, absolutely. Daily. Super helpful for me. It's about "setting my mind" and "getting out of my own head." It's about the bigger picture beyond my pain and suffering. It's about my pain and suffering being redeemed and used for good.
- EMDR. I've benefited greatly from this. I still practice EMDR principles, and they are very helpful to me.
- Massage did play a big part in releasing repressed memories from my childhood that led to massive upheaval, but also great healing.
- Grief Counseling. I've benefited greatly from this!
- Membership in a grief support group. I've led lots of groups, but I was never in one while grieving!
- Leading a grief support group. I've led multiple. Wonderful experience. I've found that having some content in my head is always good, but the key is letting people talk in a safe and somewhat controlled atmosphere.
- Supporting a cause.
- Community volunteerism.
- Working in a field related to your loved one. I ended up eventually in hospice work, so that's certainly an extension of my grief process and multiple losses.

SHARON, NATHAN'S MOTHER: LOST SON AT AGE FORTY TO SUICIDE

How has grief changed you?
I have lost family members, but losing a child has changed me. I have a hole in me that will never go away. I can hardly look at photos and past memories yet. I carry anxiety daily, that something will happen to one of my other boys. I just don't feel the same about life in general.

What has grief taught you?
It doesn't go away.

What regrets did you have regarding your loved one and how did you overcome them?
I have so many regrets as a parent. I feel guilt for decisions I made when my son was younger. Would things have been different if I had stayed married to his dad? I was not strict enough as a single parent. What made him turn to drugs and alcohol? Was it something I did?

How has your life changed since the loss?
I find it difficult to be happy. Guilt takes over and wins.

What advice could you pass on to other grieving parents?
Get help!

Have you tried any healing therapies or techniques to help you heal?
No, I have not. Sadly I have had no therapy as of yet.
I did participate in the Light Walk for suicide. It did help to see that I am not alone in this journey. There are so many who have lost loved ones to suicide.

Is there anything else you would like to add?
I have not had any grief counseling or therapy. I'm sure this would help, and I'm really not sure why I have not reached out to anyone. I hope I can find happiness at some point, but I'm not sure it's possible.

DEB, DEAN'S MOTHER: LOST SON AT AGE TWENTY-NINE TO A CAR ACCIDENT

What helped most in healing your grief?
It was a long process—years! My faith in the Lord has been the most help.

How has grief changed you?
I feel I am stronger or have disengaged my feelings, not sure which is true. I have had several losses other than my son, family and friends, so I feel almost accustomed to it. I am not sure if that's good or bad. I am hoping that I have just learned to walk through the pain quicker and easier with God.

What has grief taught you?
There is no escape from it, it is there and it's best not to stuff grief. I did it for years and it was more painful.

What regrets did you have regarding your loved one and how did you overcome them?
I regret not having spent more time together and visits. We lived in different states. It's better today, I don't rehash like I used to and have let go of resentment of his stepmother and the driver of the other vehicle.

How has your life changed since the loss?
It's forever changed, there is no going back. I value my loved ones that are here more!

What advice could you pass on to other grieving parents?
Always hold on to the fact that you will be together again for eternity. It's only a portion of our life that we are separated. If I did not have Christ and that knowledge, I don't know how I would be coping.

Have you tried any healing therapies or techniques to help you heal?
- Prayer
- Meditation
- Grief counseling
- Community volunteerism

Is there anything else you would like to add?
There is always peace to be had if we are willing to allow the healing to come in, and the peace. The Lord is my rock!

CHRISTY, ALEXIS'S MOTHER: LOST DAUGHTER AT AGE TWENTY TO A PULMONARY EMBOLISM BELIEVED TO BE CAUSED BY A BIRTH CONTROL PILL

What helped most in healing your grief?
Talking about my girl, yes, it hurts, but I also have so many amazing memories and I want all to know how great she was. Many of her friends call, text, visit at the house or we do lunch dates. Random people such as yourself who have experienced the same loss reach out to listen and talk to those who are going through the daily pain. Letting others share stories of my Sweet Pea, laughing and crying together.

How has grief changed you?
I spend more quiet time with myself, crying, reading, texting, and calling close friends. It is still a journey that I make my way through and try and do what is important to me and those I love. I never can understand how my tear ducts have never dried up, the tears flow all of the time. I'm much more understanding of others. Though it is not the pain of losing a child that they are dealing with, it is real and is pain for them. I do not compare myself to others, I'm very sympathetic.

What has grief taught you?
Spend lots of time with those you love. Being aware of not only how much they mean to me but how much I mean to them. Never shy away from showing your love to someone. I'm vulnerable and I do not hide it, if I need to cry or step away I now do.

What regrets did you have regarding your loved one and how did you overcome them?
I feel I could have been a better mom when she was little. I was not as patient as I should have been. I have read books that have helped and talked with friends. Alexis and I had a very close relationship, and I loved every moment of being her mom.

How has your life changed since the loss?
I talk with my mom more than ever, hug and tell friends and family how much I love them.

What advice could you pass on to other grieving parents?
Never stop sharing stories of your child. Don't close yourself off to those around you, be open about your grief and what you are going through.

Have you tried any healing therapies or techniques to help you heal?
I have done lots of praying, reading books relating to loss, read many articles on loss of children and parents' feelings and their advice. I work out at a gym, they are my second family. Working out releases my anger. My husband and I got our first tattoo to honor our daughter, she wanted a tattoo once she graduated college. Mine is of a Sweet Pea flower with her actual signature as the stem, placed over my heart.

Did any therapies help you, and if so, how?
Working out has helped me to get out the anger I feel. One of my closest friends said once, "We get to do this." She is so right. We get to be on Earth and have the choice every day to make ourselves better.

Is there anything else you would like to add?
The pain never goes away and that is okay; it reminds us of how much love we have for them. Do not give up ever; each day will have its ups and downs, but always remember how they would have lived and what they would have wanted for us!

TAMARA, AVENELLE'S MOTHER: LOST DAUGHTER AT AGE THIRTY-SIX WEEKS IN THE WOMB

What helped most in healing your grief?
What has helped me most in my healing is my faith in God, and talking and sharing about our daughter with other people who have lost a child. It is so amazing the power of connection and healing in talking with others who have lost a child as well. To me this is huge. It allows me to share the pain and loss I have with others who can share and understand that level of pain. I feel it has also allowed me to help others in their journey of grief—to know that someone else understands is so comforting and to talk

about your child without feeling that you are making others feel awkward. It brings such peace and comfort to the hurting. It also makes your child "real" and confirms that they existed, which is HUGE to me. Also knowing that our daughter is in heaven, healed and in no more pain, brings me such comfort. It is my faith in God that I cling to. I don't know what I would do without it. The hope and promise that Avenelle is in heaven with Jesus and someday we will reunite with and see her keeps me going. It fills my life with hope.

What has grief taught you?

Grief has taught me that life is hard. To look at each day of life with appreciation. Life is very short. We never know what will happen from moment to moment. Everyone grieves differently. For me, my heart was so broken. The hole left in my life and heart after Avenelle's death was so huge and hurt so much. There is no time table as you walk through the process. Bruce was ready to be done with crying after Avenelle's funeral, I was not.

I carried her, felt her, and loved her in my womb for eight months. It has been thirty-eight years since she died and there are still times that I will just break down for no reason. Losing Avenelle taught me to be grateful for the children who we birthed, who we could hold, love, and raise and are still here on this earth. It taught me to cling to my faith and the promise of eternal life. This promise is the hope I cling to—that someday I will hold Avenelle and be with her.

Has grief changed you?

I think it has in the sense I appreciate life more. I appreciate the children we have on this earth to hug, hold and have many memories with. I felt I was a very patient mother (most of the time). Of course, I had my moments, but I really enjoyed spending time with them. My children say they don't recall me being angry at them but when I did get angry they knew I was serious. I feel my faith is stronger. To make sense out of Avenelle's death I trust Jesus more, his death and resurrection.

I cling to the fact that God loved Avenelle so much that he took her to be with him to free her of the pain of this world. I remember my mom telling me that she and some coworkers thought it was the doctor's fault, that he could've saved Avenelle. I urged her to not continue that thought process and/or share with me as I had had those thoughts myself and it wasn't helpful and wouldn't bring Avenelle back. I do realize it was her way of grieving and trying to make sense, to blame someone. A very normal human reaction. For me, though, I needed to cling to my Lord. I believe that is when I started a deeper relationship with Jesus and my faith journey with him.

What has helped you heal?

My faith for sure. Talking with God and believing that Avenelle is in glory and joy with Jesus, in no pain and that someday I will see her again, and that our other children will get the opportunity to meet their sister. I lost my sister, mom, and dad in less than two years recently. I had a vision of my sister holding Avenelle and introducing her to my mom and dad. That gives me great comfort. Also hearing of others who have lost a child and sharing my story with them and discussing the pain of losing a child.

There is a connection and such comfort in knowing they understand the pain of losing a child, even though the stories are different there is such a huge understanding and comfort in the pain you carry. Talking about Avenelle, people remembering and asking about her, is a huge help and step in healing. To make her real and her memory alive!

We had a funeral for Avenelle, we visit her grave, we have taken our other children to see her gravestone, made a stone for her to put in a memory garden, and recently had a wall plaque made in her honor at Faith's Lodge. Faith's Lodge supports parents and families coping with the death or medically complex condition of a child in a peaceful environment to reflect on the past, renew strength for the present, and build hope for the future.

What is one thing that helped your family?

Avenelle was our first child so we didn't have other children to talk with her about. Our larger family we talk to about Avenelle and they with us. We acknowledge her birth/death day. Counting her in the number of descendants and speaking about her

What regrets did you have regarding your loved one and how did you overcome them?

The biggest regret is that we didn't get a picture of Avenelle Joy. We were so young, myself just twenty-two and my husband twenty-four. We were in shock. Her death was so unexpected, and we didn't even know what we needed or what to ask for. My dad really wanted to see her, but the funeral home discouraged him, as her skin was starting to peel away so the image wouldn't have been a pleasant one. Having a picture of her would have made her more real to our children and others. I have come to peace with this and accept that the best picture of Avenelle is in our minds. A picture would not replicate the beauty and love we felt and saw in her sweet little, lifeless body. God has helped with His comforting peace. Even though the doctors and others who knew us felt we were handling "everything" so well, I wished we would've gone through counseling. Going to counseling is more encouraged and accepted now and I feel would've helped us heal more deeply and accept Avenelle's death together as a couple. We would've understood each other's grief journey better.

How has your life changed since the loss?
Life changed as we got pregnant two months after being married. It was a great surprise but we were excited. Then when she died, our hopes, dreams were shattered. I became infertile, Bruce had to have an operation, it was a long process. We moved twice in one year, changing doctors, going through tests, medication, surgeries, etc. Our arms were empty and the desire to have a child was much greater.

We knew that having a child wouldn't change the loss and grief of losing Avenelle, but the desire to have a child was so much stronger after losing her. I feel we valued and appreciated the gift of our "live" children more. When our first son was born (and all of our children), we held our breath until we heard their first cry. Then there were tears of joy and thanks to God for the blessed gift of a live child.

What advice could you pass on to other grieving parents?
Love and respect each other's grief journey. It won't be the same, and that is okay. Approach with humble love. Speak openly and honestly about the pain you're feeling and about your child with love and compassion for each other. There is no right or wrong way. There is no timeline. Support each other and seek counseling to help you through. Grief is hard and a trained counselor can help you walk through. Join a support group to share and listen to others and their stories. It is so healing to hear of others who have lost a child and understand the pain you are feeling. Figure out a way to honor and remember your child. A beautiful way to keep them

alive. Pray and trust in God. It is my faith in God that has carried me, and us, to healing and peace.

Have you tried any healing therapies or techniques to help you heal?
- Prayer has been a HUGE technique in healing for us. Praying together and on our own. Putting our trust in God. Knowing that Avenelle is in glory with our Lord is so comforting.
- Meditation. My daily morning time with the Lord gives me such peace and healing for my soul. I don't totally understand why Avenelle was taken before we had the opportunity to meet her and know her as our child, making memories. I do find comfort in knowing that God's ways are so much better than our ways. That God loved Avenelle so much that He spared her from the pain of this life and she is in joy and glory with God and some day we will get to see her again and share in the joy!
- We were able to make a stone with Avenelle's name and birth/death date to be placed in a memorial garden for children who had died. It was beautiful. We had a service for Avenelle and made a stone to be placed where she is buried with her name and date.
- We also had a memorial plaque made for her that is on a wall at Faith's Lodge, "a place where those coping with the death or medically complex condition of a child can find hope and strength for the future."

Is there anything else you would like to add?
The death of a child, no matter the age or circumstances, is so hard. No loss is greater. And for each person who loses a child, that IS the greatest loss for that person. Be gentle with yourself, take time to grieve. Grief is so individual. Make sure to open up with love, compassion, and a listening ear to all who are grieving. Learn to ignore and laugh to yourself when people say things, in awkward moments, that may seem hurtful. They are just trying to help. There will be times that emotions seem so unbearable. In those times, acknowledge, pray, and allow yourself to work through the emotions. Talk to others. Reach out when you need. Don't be afraid to talk about your child for fear it will make others uncomfortable. Your child is a part of you and your life. They are real and should be celebrated, mourned, and shared.

JENNY, CHADWICK'S MOTHER: LOST SON AT THE AGE SIXTEEN IN A CAR ACCIDENT

What helped most in healing your grief?
Compassionate Friends Group, talking, and hearing other people's stories.

How has grief changed you?
I have lost so much joy that I feel that my personality has changed. I miss the old Jenny at times. I take more time for people, family, and friends.

What has grief taught you?
That I am a survivor!

What regrets did you have regarding your loved one and how did you overcome them?
I felt that I had all the time in the world, and that if I missed a race or an event at school I would just attend the next one. I regretted this, and overcame it with forgiveness.

How has your life changed since the loss?
I have really slowed down. I stop and smell the roses. I appreciate my family, friends, and take time for strangers to have a conversation or two. To love every minute of life.

What advice could you pass on to other grieving parents?
To not rush grief. It's a journey and takes time to heal. One minute at a time, one day at a time.

Have you tried any healing therapies or techniques to help you heal?
- Prayer.
- Meditation.
- Grief Counseling.
- Membership in a Grief Support Group.
- We had a memorial race to honor Chad at his favorite racetrack.

Did any of the above help you, and if so, how?
The above helped me to process all the events and emotions.

Is there anything else you would like to add?
There will be days that it's okay if you're not okay. There will be days that you just have to feel sorry for yourself. Allow yourself to feel, cry, laugh. It's a process, a journey.

JENNA – LOST TWO SONS, AGES SIX AND EIGHT, IN A HOUSE FIRE

How has grief changed you?
I'm not so sure that grief changed me, but the loss of my sons and everything except my husband and our cat definitely changed me. Material things are no longer as important—people and relationships are so much more important. People and experiences cannot be replaced, but my house, my furniture, my clothes and jewelry can all be replaced, except for pictures. I lost all my pictures and I still get sad over that. I no longer get angry over little things. To me, it's more important to have happiness and peace than to win an argument, to be "right." I don't like how I "feel" when I'm angry, so I choose happiness, joy, peace, and love!

What has grief taught you?
I would guess that what grief taught me (but I really don't call it grief, I call it loss) is that nothing is forever and we have a limited time on Earth, a limited time with the people we love and to make each moment count—don't waste time and energy on things you have no control over.

You have touched my life with your love, and you will live on forever in my heart. Until I take my last breath, I will miss you, my beautiful son. Forever in my heart.
—Cindy Baumann

A MOTHER'S LOVE

BY JOSEPH LANGE

The story below was written by somebody God placed in my path. Many thanks to Joseph Lange for taking the time to notice, to care, and to feel the impact of Shaun's passing.

MOST OF MY short stories deal with me growing up and surviving to be sixty-two years old and finding the humor in an oftentimes not-too-humorous world. Being able to see my daughters grow up and get married, and seeing my grandsons grow and go to college, is everything. I've had a full life. A beat-the-odds life. A no-regrets life.

With hunting season here, I was thinking about the happy times that I have experienced over forty-seven years of hunting. I thought about a time that I will recall for you in the hopes that you may find time in your busy lives to read it to your loved ones.

Thirty-three years ago, I was working in security at the hospital in Marshfield. I worked nights and was stationed at the main entrance. They were long crazy nights. I saw a lot of things come through those doors.

One evening, I saw a young girl walk past my office pushing a stroller. I noticed her face had an expression of quiet anguish, yet she managed a smile and continued down the hall. The next evening, and then the next, I saw her walking the stroller that held a little boy. I got up and opened the door as she went past and asked her if she needed a cup of coffee or if I could be of assistance in any way. Watching her walk past, so alone, pushing that child, was breaking my heart.

She was from out of town, from a tiny place up north she said, and her little boy had cancer. She was at the hospital for him to undergo a series of treatments, and the emotional stress of a young mother dealing with her child going through this horror, and being away from home, the expense and stress was incredible.

We had coffee and I listened to her relate her trials and how much she loved her little man. I had one of my don't-like-God-too-much moments, and with all the not-so-nice folks I dealt with in my job, I wondered why God gives cancer to little kids.

I didn't see the young mother after that and hoped things worked out for her and her little boy.

Fast forward to many years later.

I did most of my bowhunting along the Highway 8 corridor area, and one day I stopped into the gas station. As I was leaving, I saw a photo hanging on the wall, of a young man who appeared to be twenty-five or so, kneeling by a deer. The caption read *In Memory of Shaun Winter*.

I remembered the young mother so many years ago, her last name, and I recalled that her son's name was Shaun. I turned to the attendant and asked, "So, he didn't beat that damn cancer?"

She stated, "No, he beat it. He was killed in a hunting accident during gun season."

I felt the blood run from my face. I was floored. What the hell. "Does his mom still live around here?" I asked.

The teller didn't know but said she thought that his mom had moved away, and that was that.

I didn't hunt that day. I turned around and went home. Over the next few weeks, I was haunted by the memory of that mother and how in God's holy name her son could beat cancer and then have this happen. What kind of God would let that happen? I had to find her and have her tell me what happened. I couldn't explain it, since I had only known her for four days, but I had to know.

I located her after a lot of effort, and a bit of luck. She remembered me. At that time, I was the Director of Facilities at the hospital and she said that she had a clinic appointment soon and would stop and tell me what happened.

When I saw her coming down the hall, the memories of the young mother and her little son came flooding back to me.

She told me that she had spent many hours at the hospital involving long trips and that her son had beaten cancer. He had grown to be a strong young man and gotten married. I saw a photo of him holding his mom's hand at the top of Rib Mountain on his wedding day, and the look of love they were exchanging was heart-wrenching.

That day of the gun deer season came as all do, and although the young man wasn't a gun hunter as much as he was a fine bow hunter, Shaun decided to join the group that day for the camaraderie of being with his family. Gun hunting is a family tradition up north and Shaun was all about family.

A deer ran between Shaun and another member of the hunting party and Shaun was struck and killed.

He had graduated from UW Madison with a degree in biochemistry and was studying for his MCATs so that he could enter medical school. He was considering a specialty in pediatric oncology to help children survive cancer.

The finality of it hit me. My heart sank.

He was twenty-six. This month he would have been thirty-five.

In Loving Memory of Shaun Winter is a Facebook page that his mom started to keep the memory of her son alive. I would ask all of you who consider me a friend to go to that site and see what pain looks like:

https://www.facebook.com/groups/20238265344.

This is a real pain. Break-your-heart pain. Look at the photos. Read her comments. Sit in a quiet place—and read them. A mother's love is legendary; I know my ma loved me very much. I cannot imagine a mother loving her child more than this one.

A scholarship fund has been established in his name at UW Marathon County. I ask anybody that considers me a friend to give thought to donating to this scholarship. Any amount is welcome. This name needs to be remembered so that his story can go on being told.

Shaun L. Winter Memorial Scholarship
https://greatstartswithu.org/how-to-give/

Mothers, please, take time this fall to not just mention it. Sit your family down. Look them in their eyes. Get their attention. *Tell them this story.*

CINDY BAUMANN is an entrepreneur, grief coach, and writer. She was a partner of a multi-million-dollar advertising agency for twenty-five years. She sold the Central Wisconsin business a few years after it was awarded a Wausau Region Chamber of Commerce Small Business of the Year in 2016, to focus on writing and grief support.

From a Midwest farm girl to a rising executive, her fast-track life came to a screeching halt in 2007 when she had to deal with the unthinkable, which left her with PTSD. Years of struggling to survive—and unraveling past tragedies—led to a journey of self-discovery and enlightenment, along with a new career focus. Where she once saw courage as being fearless in the face of big business deals, she now believes it's found in helping others battle the darkness as she did.

Cindy lives with her husband in Bonita Springs, Florida, and spends her summers in Northern Wisconsin. They are lucky to have their children and family spend time with them in both locations. She has a degree in marketing and is a certified grief and life coach. Her mission is to keep telling a deeply personal story of grief and survival to inspire others and show the pathways to hope and healing.

Cindy is proof that hard work and faith in God can move mountains, and that peace and happiness are possible after tragedy strikes.

HEALING SCRIPTURES

Many Scriptures have helped me in times of anguish. Speaking these verses aloud, or other positive affirmations and inspirational words, can be a powerful way of strengthening ourselves. There is something about saying the words rather than just reading them that carries weight and authority. Here are some of my favorites:

Psalm 147:3
He heals the brokenhearted and bandages their wounds.

1 Peter 5:7
Give all your worries and cares to God, for he cares about you.

Matthew 5:4
God blesses those who mourn, for they will be comforted.

Psalm 34:18
The Lord is close to the brokenhearted; he rescues those whose spirits are crushed.

1 Corinthians: 13
Three things will last forever—faith, hope, and love—and the greatest of these is love.

Revelation 21:4
He will wipe every tear from their eyes, and there will be no more death or sorrow or crying or pain. All these things are gone forever.

Isaiah 41:10
Don't be afraid, for I am with you. Don't be discouraged, for I am your God. I will strengthen you and help you. I will hold you up with my victorious right hand.

Romans 8:18
Yet what we suffer now is nothing compared to the glory he will reveal to us later.

John 16:22
So you have sorrow now, but I will see you again; then you will rejoice, and no one can rob you of that joy.

Psalm 9:9
The Lord is a shelter for the oppressed, a refuge in times of trouble.

2 Corinthians 1:3
All praise to God, the Father of our Lord Jesus Christ. God is our merciful Father and the source of all comfort.

Isaiah 25:8
He will swallow up death forever! The Sovereign LORD will wipe away all tears. He will remove forever all insults and mockery against his land and people. The LORD has spoken!

Isaiah 43:2
When you go through deep waters, I will be with you. When you go through rivers of difficulty, you will not drown. When you walk through the fire of oppression, you will not be burned up; the flames will not consume you.

Matthew 11:28
Then Jesus said, "Come to me, all of you who are weary and carry heavy burdens, and I will give you rest."

Psalm 23:4
Even when I walk through the darkest valley, I will not be afraid, for you are close beside me. Your rod and your staff protect and comfort me.

Psalm 126:5
Those who plant in tears will harvest with shouts of joy.

John 16:20
I tell you the truth, you will weep and mourn over what is going to happen to me, but the world will rejoice. You will grieve, but your grief will suddenly turn to wonderful joy.

ACKNOWLEDGMENTS

Deepest thanks to . . .

God and Shaun
For working together from heaven to inspire me to tell my story and help others on their grief journey. Thank you, God, for walking with me. Sometimes you were behind giving me subtle nudges to keep moving forward and other times you were beside me holding my hand with such grace.

Special thanks to the following important people in my life

My husband (Kevin) and children (Ryan, Jordan, and Justin)
For having faith in me and knowing I still loved them as we walked through the darkness and despair of grief.

Maria, my daughter-in-law
For your continued support and love—you are like a daughter to me.

Braelynn, my granddaughter
For giving me a new outlook on life and blessing all of us when we needed it most.

My Parents
For always being available when we needed you. You helped me survive
this loss. I couldn't have made it without the love and support you gave
us. For the first couple of years after Shaun died, you stopped in to visit us
every Sunday. It didn't matter if we were home or at the lake—you would
find us and give your time. I am grateful beyond measure for everything
you did. Thank you, Mom and Dad. I know how hard this was while you
were hurting so deeply. I love and admire both of you.

Julia, my daughter-in-law
For being Shaun's wife, for loving him as you did, for being the best thing
that ever happened to him. You were his soul mate. He departed this Earth
having received and given true love, a beautiful gift. You will forever own a
piece of my heart.

Fran, Shaun's father
For helping me bring our precious son into the world. We shared a
significant loss and have learned to talk about it, which is very healing. On
the extra-hard days, we lift each other by sharing encouraging messages.
In my heart, I know Shaun was instrumental in making us supportive of
one another. He was a peacemaker, and always happiest when everybody
got along. We will continue to uphold what Shaun would have wanted, by
honoring him with forgiveness and acceptance.

My Siblings and Other Family
For all the care you showed to Shaun during his life, and for keeping his
memory alive with your own families. He was looked up to by so many
nieces, nephews, and cousins. Thanks to all who loved him.

Ron & Elba, Julia's parents
For loving Shaun like a son.

Friends
For not giving up on me and continuing to support us on this difficult
journey.

Frances (Frankie) Key, editor
For your talented editing, contribution of ideas, compassion, and commitment to my story. Thanks so much for your help in making this dream become a reality.

Robert Holden, PhD
For your kind words of encouragement that helped on my grief journey. Your powerful statement "Your grief deserves your attention, your patience, and your compassion" could not have been more true. You were right—I had to learn to continue my relationship with "the spiritual being that came into the world as my child" and to "trust the unseen hands" that led me through the darkness.

Jan Warner, M.S. in Counseling, beta reader
For graciously becoming a beta reader of an earlier draft of my book, providing valuable insights, and being kind enough to read the final version.

Christy Distler, proofreader
For your attention to detail and responsive follow-up.

Yvonne Parks, cover design
For respecting my opinion and allowing me to be involved in the design of the cover.

Karla Swita, beta reader
For encouraging me to tell my story as well as reviewing my manuscript and offering helpful content suggestions.

Rick Jass, MA, Licensed Professional Counselor
For encouraging me to keep going with EMDR treatments, listening with compassion, and helping us save our marriage.

Father Steve, my parish priest
For not judging me and supporting me on my spiritual journey.

Nan and Gary Zastrow – Wings, a grief education ministry
Thanks for validating that I wasn't going crazy and supporting me on my path to healing.

Dr. Ivan Schaller
For seeing I needed help when I didn't know how to ask for it.

Dick Lange, friend and author
For telling me to "keep writing."

Contributors to the chapter In the Words of Others
For honestly sharing your experiences with other parents who have lost a child. Some of you walked beside me on my journey through grief and others, I met along the way. To all, I'm deeply grateful.

Jack
Janelle
Rosanna
Tamara
Nan
Gary
Katie
Mark
Stephanie
Sue
Dan
Brian
Paige
Wendy
Rev. Riddley
Gary
Sharon
Deb
Christy
Tamara
Jenny
Jenna

All the moms and dads who have lost children.

The authors who have inspired me with their books and advice.

Many people have touched my life over the years. Some were present for a short time and were meant to cross my path briefly. Others have been by my side for years. I believe people come into our lives for all sorts of reasons. Thank you, one and all, for making the world a more loving and beautiful place.

In Memory of My Brother, Terrance (Terry) Harold Mustard

August 19, 1962 – November 27, 2018

REFERENCES

Merriam-Webster.com Dictionary, s.v. "regret," accessed July 20, 2021, https://www.merriam-webster.com/dictionary/regret.

Byock, Ira. *The Four Things That Matter Most: A Book about Living*. New York: Free Press, 2004.

Chapman, Gary. *The Five Love Languages: The Secret to Love that Lasts*. Chicago: Northfield Publishing, 2004.

Conner, Janet. *Soul Writing: How to Activate and Listen to the Extraordinary Voice Within*. Berkeley, CA: Conari Press, 2009.

Holden, Robert. *Be Happy!: Release the power of Happiness in YOU*. Carlsbad, CA: Hay House, 2009.

Holden, Robert. *Finding Love Everywhere: 67½ Wisdom Poems and Meditations*. Carlsbad, CA: Hay House, 2020.

Holden, Robert. *Holy Shift!: 365 Daily Meditations from a Course in Miracles*. Carlsbad, CA: Hay House, 2011.

Holden, Robert. *Loveability: Knowing How to Love and Be Loved*. Carlsbad, CA: Hay House, 2013.

Holden, Robert. *Shift Happens!: How to Live an Inspired Life...Starting Right Now*. Carlsbad, CA: Hay Hous